ARIZONA

WEEKEND *Rock*

trad and sport
routes from 5.0
to 5.10a

ARIZONA

LON ABBOTT

THE MOUNTAINEERS BOOKS

THE MOUNTAINEERS BOOKS
is the nonprofit publishing arm of The Mountaineers Club, an organization founded in 1906 and dedicated to the exploration, preservation, and enjoyment of outdoor and wilderness areas.

1001 SW Klickitat Way, Suite 201, Seattle, WA 98134

© 2006 by Lon Abbott

First edition, 2006

Manufactured in the United States of America

Acquiring Editor: Christine Hosler
Project Editor: Mary Metz
Copy Editor: Colin Chisholm
Cover and Book Design: The Mountaineers Books
Layout: Mayumi Thompson
Cartographer: Moore Creative Design
Photographer: All photos by author unless otherwise noted.

Cover photograph: *Chance Traub climbing* Trouble in Paradise—*Rupley Towers*
Frontispiece: *Matt Moss on the stellar first pitch of* Magnolia Thunder Pussy *at Granite Mountain*
Page 5: *Chance Traub leading* R-3 *at Mount Lemmon*
Page 6: *McNeill Mann climbing* Dislocation Direct *at Granite Mountain*

Library of Congress Cataloging-in-Publication Data
Abbott, Lon, 1963-
  Weekend Rock Arizona / by Lon Abbott.
    p. cm.
  ISBN 0-89886-965-X (alk. paper)
  1. Rock climbing—Arizona—Guidebooks. I. Title.
  GV199.42.A7A235 2006
  796.52'2309791—dc22
                                        2006005482

✪ Printed on recycled paper

Contents

Dedication 7

*Choose Your Destination
Chart   9*

Acknowledgments 11

Introduction 13

DRAGOON MOUNTAINS 25
Cochise Stronghold West 29
Isle of You 50

MOUNT LEMMON 55
Windy Point 59
Ridgeline 76

QUEEN CREEK 83
The Mine Area 87
The Pond Area 99

PINNACLE PEAK 109
The Wedge 113
AMC Boulder 117
Summit Pinnacles 119
Y-Crack Boulder 122
Cactus Flower East 124

MCDOWELL MOUNTAINS 129
Sven Slab 135
Gardener's Wall 140
Tom's Thumb 145

GRANITE MOUNTAIN 155
Swamp Slabs 160
Front Porch Area 171

THUMB BUTTE 179
West Side Climbs—Kitty Cracks
Area 183
South Side Climbs 184

SEDONA 199
Goliath 204
Queen Victoria 210
Streaker Spire 213
The Mace 216
Four Flying Apaches 220
Bell Rock 224
Mars Attacks! 226

OAK CREEK OVERLOOK 231

JACKS CANYON 253
Casino Cliffs 256
Cracker Jack Cliffs 263
High Life Wall 271

APPENDIXES 273
A: Additional Resources and Land Management Information 273
B: Routes by Difficulty 276
C: Routes by Quality 279
About the UIAA/Table of Difficulties 282
Index 283

THIS BOOK IS DEDICATED TO

My family–Thank you, Terri, for all of your love and support. Logan and Kailas, I hope the future holds for us many wonderful days in the outdoors together;

Roger Briggs–A gifted climber and teacher;

Every one of my climbing partners–
You have profoundly influenced my life. Thank you.

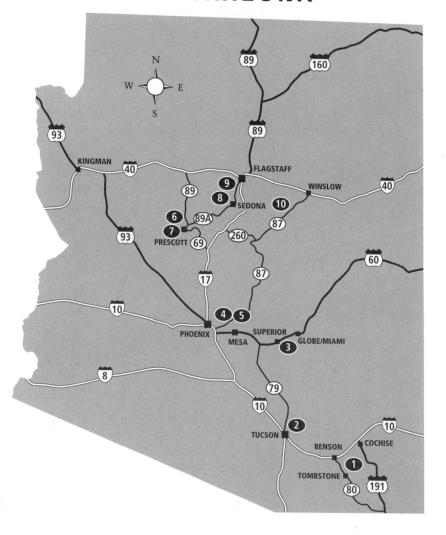

1 Dragoon Mountains
2 Mount Lemmon
3 Queen Creek
4 Pinnacle Peak
5 McDowell Mountains
6 Granite Mountain
7 Thumb Butte
8 Sedona
9 Oak Creek Overlook
10 Jacks Canyon

ARIZONA

CHOOSE YOUR DESTINATION CHART

Destination	Drive time from Tucson	Drive time from Phoenix	Drive time from Flagstaff	Approach times	Climbing season	Rock type	Climbing type
Dragoon Mountains	2 hours	3½ hours	5½ hours	5 minutes to 1 hour	October to April	Granite	Multi-pitch trad, sport
Granite Mountain	3½ hours	1½ hours	1½ hours	1½ hours	July to February	Granite	Multi-pitch trad
Jacks Canyon	4 hours	2½ hours	1½ hours	5–15 minutes	Year-round	Limestone	Sport
McDowell Mountains	2 hours	½ hour	2¼ hours	5–50 minutes	October to April	Granite	Trad, bolted slab
Mount Lemmon	½ hour	2 hours	4 hours	Roadside to 15 minutes	Year-round	Gneiss and Granite	Trad, sport
Oak Creek Overlook	4 hours	2 hours	20 minutes	10 minutes	Year-round	Basalt	Trad cracks
Pinnacle Peak	2 hours	½ hour	2 hours	10–15 minutes	October to April	Granite	Trad, bolted slab
Queen Creek	2 hours	1 hour	3 hours	5–15 minutes	September to April	Welded tuff	Sport, a few cracks
Sedona	3½ hours	1½ hours	45 minutes	20 minutes to 1 hour	September to May	Sandstone	Multi-pitch trad spires
Thumb Butte	3½ hours	1½ hours	1½ hours	30 minutes	July to February	Volcanic latite	Trad

Acknowledgments

This book would not have been possible without the help and support of many people. First and foremost I'd like to thank Terri Cook for her endless support and for making it possible for me to spend the time required to create a book. Thanks are due to Laura Plaut for her extensive help in the early stages of this project. Thank you to all of the climbers who shared a rope with me during this project or who shared their knowledge and expertise. A partial list includes the following: David Lovejoy, Brian Ford, Steve Munsell, Matt Moss, Jonathon Reckling, Phil Latham, and all the participants in the 2005 Prescott College Rock Climbing and Geology course. I am especially indebted to the two most indefatigable of my reconnaissance partners, Chance Traub and Kate McEwen. Thanks also to Charlie Crocker, Charity Kahn, and Chance Traub for use of their photos. Thanks to all of the people at The Mountaineers Books who make these guides a reality, with special thanks to Cassandra Conyers, who helped get me started on this project, and to Christine Hosler, Mary Metz, and Colin Chisholm, who guided the manuscript with helpful and steady hands.

Introduction

Arizona is a climber's paradise. Few states possess such a diverse collection of climbing areas that offer visitors outstanding year-round climbing. Thanks to Arizona's exceptionally varied geography and geology, climbing venues exist at elevations as low as 3000 feet and as high as 7000 feet, providing escape from the chill of winter and sanctuary from searing summer heat. The climbing itself is as diverse as the climates. Multi-pitch granite cracks and slabs, pocketed sport climbs on welded tuff and limestone, hand-friendly basalt cracks and corners, and soaring sandstone spires provide climbers with all the variety the sport has to offer. This fantastic climbing unfolds at locations easily accessible from urban areas, yet a world away from the rat race. The settings for Arizona's climbing areas are diverse and beautiful: serene pine forests, flower-studded oak woodlands, and saguaro-strewn deserts. Most of these areas lie within vast tracts of public land that offer other enjoyable diversions, from hiking and mountain biking to hanging out in quiet campgrounds or sharing a meal with friends.

Arizona has its share of desperate test pieces, routes that seem to require levitation just to get off the ground! But its climbing areas are also replete with classic routes at more reasonable grades, and climbers who find 5.0–5.9 (or 5.10a for sport climbs) more to their liking can choose from many wonderful lines. The goal of this book is to get you to the best places for climbing the most worthwhile 5.0–5.10a routes in Arizona.

HOW TO USE THIS BOOK

This book will provide you with all the information you need to spend several enjoyable weekends climbing and recreating at ten of Arizona's best climbing areas. I have selected these areas because each hosts many enjoyable, high-quality moderate climbs, and each is easily accessible for a day or weekend. Together they represent an amazing diversity of climbing styles and beautiful natural settings. The climbs listed in this book represent the best of what Arizona has to offer weekend climbers.

Along with maps directing you to each climbing area and to the

Jonathon Reckling leading the airy third pitch of Four Flying Apaches *at Sedona*

routes, each area description includes a "beta box" in which you will find the following:

- Driving instructions and travel time from Flagstaff, Phoenix, and Tucson
- Approach time to climbs
- Weather, elevation, and climbing season
- Regulations and access information
- Camping and lodging
- Nearest food, water, and supplies
- Types of climbing available (sport, multi-pitch, etc.) and gear recommendations
- Emergency services
- Kid- and dog-friendly information

I have also included overview photographs to help orient you to the area. Every climb is shown on a photograph of the crag. Written descriptions accompany these visual aids for every route. The descriptions give you a sense of the climbing style to expect, help keep you on route, and list any special gear requirements. I've tried to provide detailed information without giving you a paint-by-numbers description of the climbing itself, thereby preserving the wonderful feeling of discovering a route's mysteries for the first time.

READING THE ROUTE PHOTOS

Each route is illustrated on a photograph of the cliff. The legend on page 15 shows the complete list of symbols used on the photographs. Routes are shown as solid lines. Bolts are depicted by an x, and belay or rappel anchors are shown using xx. Rappel stations are shown with a down arrow indicating the rappel direction and length. Fixed pi-ns are denoted with a "p." Route numbers shown at the base of each climb correspond to the route numbers listed in the accompanying climb descriptions. For multi-pitch climbs, the top of each pitch is noted with the pitch number enclosed by a circle.

RATING SYSTEM FOR DIFFICULTY, QUALITY, AND SERIOUSNESS OF CLIMBS

I've included ratings for difficulty, seriousness, and quality in order to help you select the climbs most likely to provide you with a fun and safe climbing experience.

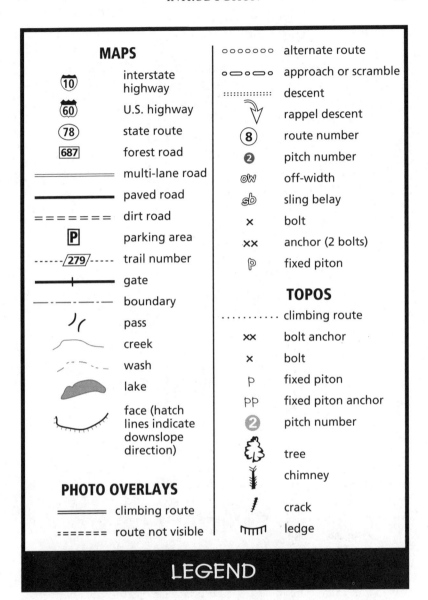

MAPS

(10)	interstate highway
(60)	U.S. highway
(78)	state route
[687]	forest road
═══════	multi-lane road
──────	paved road
═══════	dirt road
[P]	parking area
----/279/----	trail number
──┼──	gate
─ · ─ · ─ · ─	boundary
)(	pass
⌒	creek
- · - · -	wash
◗	lake
⌣	face (hatch lines indicate downslope direction)

PHOTO OVERLAYS

═══	climbing route
══════	route not visible

○○○○○○○	alternate route
○⬭○⬭○	approach or scramble
:::::::::::::::	descent
↓	rappel descent
(8)	route number
❷	pitch number
⍵	off-width
sb	sling belay
×	bolt
××	anchor (2 bolts)
℗	fixed piton

TOPOS

· · · · · · · · · ·	climbing route
××	bolt anchor
×	bolt
p	fixed piton
pp	fixed piton anchor
❷	pitch number
🌳	tree
⍦	chimney
∤	crack
�	ledge

LEGEND

Difficulty Ratings

The difficulty of climbs in this book is rated using the Yosemite Decimal System, which is the standard North American rating system. Class difficulty may be understood as follows:

Class 1: Walking on flat, easy terrain.

Class 2: Trail walking with occasional uneven surfaces, boulders, roots, etc.

Class 3: Scrambling. May require using hands as well as feet in some sections, but won't require a rope, even for beginners.

Class 4: Fourth-class terrain isn't technically difficult, but it will require the use of hands and feet and is committing enough that a misstep could result in injury or death. It is appropriate to consider using a rope on fourth-class terrain.

Class 5: This is what most people think of as technical rock climbing, with a rope and belay procedures to protect against falls. The climber uses the rope for protection but not for upward progress; you don't hang on the rope unless you fall. This style of climbing is known as "free climbing." All of the routes listed in this book are fifth-class rock climbs. Within class 5, difficulty is further divided by decimal points, 5.0–5.15. A further sublevel uses letters "a" through "d," beginning at 5.10. At lower grades it is not uncommon to see a "+" or "-" to indicate further refinement.

Class 6: These are climbs that require a rope and gear placements to aid in upward progress. Aid climbing uses ratings from A0 to A5. On A0 climbs, the climber hangs or "tensions" off one piece of fixed gear, such as a bolt or piton. It is very easy to do. A1 to A5 become progressively more difficult and dangerous. This book includes only one aid climb, *What's My Line* (A0), in the Dragoon Mountains.

The focus of this book is on climbs 5.10a and below. For traditional climbs, meaning those in which you place your own protection, I've covered only climbs 5.9 and below. Sport climbs rely exclusively on bolts permanently fixed to the rock during the first ascents. Because sport climbs that have been thoughtfully bolted usually provide a safe venue for pushing one's limits, this guide covers sport climbs up to 5.10a. In a few cases I've noted the presence of slightly more difficult climbs that are classic or that can be easily top-roped.

Remember that no climb is inherently safe. You must always assess the route, your preparation for it, and the conditions at the time of your ascent to determine whether you can safely ascend a given route on a given day. No guidebook author can ensure that all potential hazards have been mentioned for all climbs.

Keeping in mind the cautions listed above, it is reasonable for someone who has never been climbing before to climb at the 5.0–5.6 grade (and enjoy themselves in the process!), assuming that they are climbing with an experienced partner who leads the climbs or sets up the top ropes.

Climbing at the 5.7–5.9 range requires a substantial amount of skill and experience, particularly for longer, more committing routes that require the use of gear for protection. Leading a climb at any grade requires specialized training and experience that you should obtain through a climbing class from a reputable climbing guide or school. Consult with the staff at your local climbing gym or gear shop to locate a reputable climbing instructor. Climbing outside is quite different from climbing at the gym, even at sport climbing venues. When you consider the different styles that traditional climbing requires, such as hand jamming and chimneying, gym climbers will typically find themselves perplexed when they first climb at a place like Granite Mountain or Oak Creek Overlook. If you are an experienced gym climber but haven't climbed outside, it is prudent to begin on climbs considerably below your typical gym limit,

Charlie Crocker leaning over the void on the final pitch of The Mace *in Sedona*

and with a climbing partner who is experienced on real rock.

Bear in mind that difficulty ratings are highly subjective. Each area carries its own standard, and the rating of a particular climb will depend on—among other things—the era in which the route was established; the skill, mood, and judgment of the first ascensionist; the style of climbing; and the culture of the particular climbing area. You will find, for instance, that ratings at Granite Mountain, a mostly traditional area developed in the 1970s, tend to be significantly stiffer than ratings at Jacks Canyon, an area developed by and for sport climbers in the 1990s. I have generally followed the previously published difficulty ratings, but I have at times noted when ratings seem to me to be either particularly soft or stiff.

As a general rule, it is prudent to start below your normal performance level and work your way up each time you climb at a new area. Also, common sense dictates that you take not only the rating of the route but also the environment into account. In other words, just because you've climbed 5.10 in a gym does not mean that five pitches of 5.7 is safe to jump on when a storm is brewing in the west.

Seriousness of Routes

A few of the routes in this guide have an "R" after the decimal rating, which means that the leader must negotiate unusually long sections without adequate protection. A long fall with serious or fatal consequences is possible on any climb, but the possibility is greater on climbs with longer runouts. Climbs without an "R" rating provide the competent leader with protection possibilities at closer intervals. I have used "TR" to designate climbs that are readily top-roped, and "Sport" to designate sport routes (with the exception of Jacks Canyon, where all routes are sport).

Climbs are rated not only by class (5.6, 5.7, etc.) but also by grade, an indicator of the commitment and time needed for a competent team to complete the climb. The higher the grade, the more committing the climb, and hence the more serious it may become in the event of an accident or inclement weather.

Grade I: 1–3 hours
Grade II: 3–4 hours
Grade III: 4–6 hours
Grade IV–VI: A long, full day or more for a competent and efficient team

Unless otherwise noted, climbs in this guide are Grade I or II. The only areas in this book with Grade III climbs are Cochise Stronghold, Granite Mountain, and Sedona; and the Grade IIIs at these areas have been identified with the appropriate grade designation. There are no Grade IV, V, or VI climbs in this book.

Quality of Climbs

As this book is a select guide, I have only included high-quality climbs. I recommend all of the climbs listed here, but to help guide you to the best of the best, I've used a three-star system to designate exceptional climbs. A few routes haven't received any stars. They are still worth doing, but their quality may not be as fine as those I have highlighted.

★: routes that most climbers will find enjoyable

★★: routes of high quality that most climbers will eagerly repeat if given the chance

★★★: routes generally acknowledged as classics. Don't miss climbing these!

Whenever possible I have noted the first ascent party for each route and the date of the first ascent, as well as details on the first free ascent, if applicable. However, this information was not always available to me. In these cases there will be no first ascent information listed below the climb's name. My apologies to route pioneers whom I have neglected to name.

CLIMBING ETHICS/ETIQUETTE

The areas included in this book are popular, and you can expect to be sharing space with other climbers and outdoor enthusiasts. Observing a few simple rules of etiquette will not only make the experience more enjoyable for all, but also will help to ensure continued access to these wonderful areas.

- Use established access trails.
- Pack out what you pack in (including chalk and tape).
- Dispose of human waste properly.
- Be mindful of your noise level.
- Do not monopolize a climb; be aware of others who may be waiting.
- Be thoughtful of the safety of those around and below you.

KEY HEALTH AND SAFETY ISSUES

Climbing is an inherently risky endeavor. Regardless of where you climb, it is always advisable to wear your helmet, stay current on rescue protocols, and let someone know where you are going. As with all wilderness activities, it is wise to carry basic survival essentials. The Mountaineers recommends that you throw the following essential items in your pack when you head off on an adventure:

THE TEN ESSENTIALS: A SYSTEMS APPROACH

1. Navigation (map and compass)
2. Sun protection (sunglasses and sunscreen)
3. Insulation (extra clothing)

4. Illumination (headlamp or flashlight)
5. First-aid supplies
6. Fire (firestarter and matches/lighter)
7. Repair kit and tools (including knife)
8. Nutrition (extra food)
9. Hydration (extra water)
10. Emergency shelter

Safety concerns specific to Arizona focus primarily on heat and prickly desert flora and fauna. Arizona's beautiful, sunny weather makes for appealing year-round climbing. Sun, however, also causes dehydration, heat exhaustion, and sunstroke. Be sure to carry plenty of water, food, and sunscreen year-round, but particularly in the summer. Drink a lot of fluids and make sure that you eat and drink to maintain the electrolyte balance in your body.

All that said, don't let Arizona's sunny reputation fool you into thinking that you can always get by with a T-shirt and shorts. It can get bitterly cold, well below freezing during winter and spring, particularly at higher elevations. Winter snow is not uncommon at places like Oak Creek Overlook and Granite Mountain, and snow is possible at any of the areas listed in this book. Finally, please respect all of the prickly flora and fauna that make their home in the Arizona deserts. Regardless of elevation, you will encounter an abundance of cacti, and it is good to keep an eye out for snakes and scorpions. Should you be bitten or stung, seek medical care immediately. Cacti inhabit some of the ledges on routes listed in this book, so don't pull up onto a ledge blindly! Oak Creek Overlook seems to be most generously endowed with such ledge guardians. Also, Thumb Butte, Oak Creek Overlook, and Pinnacle Peak seem to have a surplus of wasps and bees.

From July through September, Arizona is visited by the monsoon, with its violent thunderstorms. Lightning strikes and flash floods are real hazards during this season. The introductory materials for

Arizona vegetation is usually armed with ample spiny protection.

each climbing area give you more specific details on what to expect from the weather.

In Arizona, each county sheriff is responsible for search and rescue operations. In the event that you have an emergency and are not able to evacuate yourself and your climbing party, a 911 operator will be able to connect you with the appropriate search and rescue personnel. Have the following information for the 911 operator: the location of the incident, the nature of the problem, the number of victims, and the types of injuries. Cell phones are helpful—sometimes—but they will not get reliable service in many of the areas listed in this guide. When making a 911 call, *always hang up last.* Make sure that the operator has all of the information necessary to help you.

WEATHER AND CLIMATE

As mentioned above, Arizona's weather is diverse and depends on elevation. Spring and fall offer the most comfortable climbing temperatures at every area described in this book, although spring offers a greater chance of rain. The lower-elevation areas, such as Pinnacle Peak and the McDowell

The summer monsoon brings patchy but violent thunderstorms that present a serious hazard.

Areas such as Queen Creek offer family-friendly fun.

Mountains, usually provide comfortable winter climbing, but even these areas can be cold and windy. Likewise, the high-elevation areas—such as Mount Lemmon, Granite Mountain, and Oak Creek Overlook—can be enjoyable for winter climbing, as they often enjoy long periods of clear, sunny winter days. That said, don't expect good weather anywhere: always check the forecast before you travel.

Summer is hot in Arizona regardless of the elevation, but the higher areas can be quite reasonable, with temperatures in the 80s. The lower-elevation areas are generally not friendly to man or beast at high noon in midsummer, with temperatures commonly north of 100 degrees, but if you are desperate for a bit of summer climbing, you can emulate lifelong Phoenicians and get out early in the morning for a few pleasant pitches at Pinnacle Peak or the McDowells.

GEAR: STANDARD RACK/SITE-SPECIFIC NEEDS

Unless otherwise noted, you may expect that a standard rack—including a single set of stoppers and camming devices, runners, and a 60-meter rope—will suffice for all climbs. I've tried to list any special gear requirements, such as large cams, where they are needed. My notation refers to specific gear, such as a #4 Camalot, small Alien, or RPs (steel or brass micronuts). Other brands that serve the same purpose are fine as well. Areas with an abundance of bolted sport routes (such as Jacks Canyon and Queen Creek) may be enjoyed with nothing more than a rope and a dozen quickdraws. Areas endowed with many long crack routes often require more gear. A typical Granite Mountain, Sedona, or Cochise Stronghold rack will usually include a double set of cams. A few routes require two ropes for rappels.

KIDS AND DOGS

Each section will give a brief word or two about whether this is a place that is well-suited for your kids and your dogs.

A NOTE ABOUT SAFETY

Safety is an important concern in all outdoor activities. No guidebook can alert you to every hazard or anticipate the limitations of every reader. Therefore, the descriptions of roads, trails, routes, and natural features in this book are not guarantees that a particular place or excursion will be safe for your party. When you follow any of the routes described in this book, you assume responsibility for your own safety. Under normal conditions, such excursions require the usual attention to traffic, road and trail conditions, weather, terrain, the capabilities of your party, and other factors. Keeping informed on current conditions and exercising common sense are the keys to a safe, enjoyable outing.

—*The Mountaineers Books*

Dragoon Mountains

The central Dragoon Mountains boast a 10-mile-long spine studded with hundreds of granite domes and towers up to 900 feet tall, a strikingly ragged profile visible far and wide throughout southeastern Arizona. The complex topography was the perfect hiding place for the Apache chief Cochise and his warriors during their numerous raiding forays during the 1860s and 70s. The range is named for the dragoons of the U.S. cavalry who were sent by the U.S. government to rid the Arizona Territory of the Apache threat. The cavalry never caught Cochise, and he died of natural causes in 1874. He was buried in Cochise Stronghold, in the heart of this granite labyrinth. Many people have searched for his grave, spurred on by their sense of history or by the rumors of treasure buried with the chief, but the site remains undiscovered.

This craggy topography that so frustrates would-be treasure hunters is a paradise for rock climbers. Many lifetimes of climbing lie in wait for those up to the challenge of routefinding, bushwhacking, and stout climbing that most of the rocks demand. Climbing in the Dragoons has an air of adventure and mystery. The southern Arizona climbing fraternity guards that mystery jealously; hundreds of climbs have been done over the years, but only a handful are well documented in easily accessible literature.

The secret of Dragoon climbing was

The rappel off The Whale *is as exhilarating as the climbs.*

closely held for so long that even today the area is not terribly well-known outside Arizona, despite the fact that it may be Arizona's best climbing area and offers some of the best winter climbing weather in the United States. While routes have been done throughout the range, most climbing in the Dragoons concentrates in four main areas: the East and West Strongholds, Sheepshead, and the Isle of You. Cochise Stronghold East, that part of the Stronghold best accessed from the east side of the range, was the first area developed, and it offers a wealth of outstanding moderate climbs that aren't covered in this guide. The West Stronghold, covered here, offers an even greater concentration of climbs between 5.6–5.9, with the added advantage of somewhat shorter and less complex approaches. Sheepshead, also known as the Southwest Stronghold, is a bastion of true adventure climbing, with bold routes that ascend the largest domes in the Dragoons. The most recently developed area is the Isle of You, a Dragoon anomaly in that it is pure sport climbing, with plenty of bolts and a 5-minute approach.

For logistical reasons, I've opted to concentrate on the West Stronghold

and Isle of You, omitting the East Stronghold and Sheepshead. It takes well over 2 hours to drive between the East and West Strongholds, so they are very much separate destinations. Sheepshead is close to the Isle of You, but its routes have a more serious flavor that makes them best suited for climbers who have already gotten a feel for Dragoon climbing. If you can't get enough of Dragoon climbing, Bob Kerry's *Backcountry Rockclimbing in Southern Arizona* is a great resource for routes in the areas not covered here, as well as for many more excellent routes in the West Stronghold.

All Dragoon climbing is on the exquisite Stronghold granite, a geologically young intrusion of magma that solidified 22–28 million years ago. It is cut by many joints that weather rapidly, leaving behind the maze of fins and domes separated by narrow corridors that make the area so remarkable. The clean faces of the rocks at Isle of You formed along some of these joints. Trad Rock, which hosts all of Isle of You's 5.10a and under routes, is 165 feet tall, offering long routes for a sport area. The face is nicely textured, providing interesting sequences that will delight face climbers. The massive walls of the West Stronghold offer climbs that range from one to five pitches in length. Many of these climbs utilize striking, Yosemite-like cracks of all sizes, but the most distinctive aspect of Stronghold climbing is the abundance of humongous chickenheads. As at granite areas worldwide, these chickenheads result from the differential erosion of the rock, but here they seem to achieve their most developed form. Many a multi-pitch wall at the Stronghold is a veritable sea of chickenheads, offering surprisingly moderate and often boltless ascents of some improbable-looking faces. *What's My Line*, undoubtedly the most famous 5.6 climb in the state, offers the archetype of the genre. Cochise chickenhead climbing takes some getting used to, but once you have the hang of it, it often proves addictive.

There is a special beauty and mystery to this enchanting place. Please enjoy it responsibly, and take special pains to keep it wild.

DRAGOON MOUNTAIN BETA

Drive time from Tucson ▲ 2 hours
Drive time from Phoenix ▲ 3½ hours
Drive time from Flagstaff ▲ 5½ hours
Getting there: Almost all climbers will approach the Dragoon Mountains from the north along I-10. Depart I-10 at exit 303 in the town of Benson and travel south on SR 80 toward Tombstone. Travel 24 miles

to milepost 315 (just 3 miles before Tombstone) and turn left onto the clearly marked Middlemarch Road. This is a good gravel road suitable for passenger cars. After 10 miles turn left onto Forest Road 687, clearly signed to the West Stronghold. You enter the national forest here. To reach the Isle of You continue 2.1 miles on FR 687 and turn right on an unmarked road immediately after crossing a cattleguard. This road dead-ends at a nice camping area immediately below the climbing cliff after 0.4 mile.

To reach the camping area for the West Stronghold, drive to the end of FR 687. This road is usually okay for two-wheel-drive vehicles, but it has some rough patches that can become impassable for low-clearance vehicles after bad weather. From the junction with Middlemarch Road, drive 7.4 miles on FR 687, roughly paralleling the range crest and passing the Isle of You turnoff, to a fence that blocks access to the Dragoon Mountain Ranch subdivision. A windmill provides a landmark here. FR 687 veers right, paralleling the fence line. Continue another 3 miles (10.4 miles total from Middlemarch Road) to the road's end. A sign for Forest Trail 279 marks the end of the road. There are a number of unmarked forks off FR 687 in the first 7.4 miles, but the main road is usually obvious and is always the fork that parallels the range crest. The parking area for climbs in the Warpath Dome area is reached before the end of the road. See the approach directions under that section.

Approach: The climbs at the Isle of You are reached via an easy 5-minute stroll. The approaches to Stronghold climbs are all strenuous and vary from 20 minutes to 1 hour.

Season and Elevation: The Isle of You lies at about 5000 feet. The camping area for the West Stonghold is at 5100 feet, and the climbs there all lie between 5600–6500 feet. Climbing is best here from fall through spring. The Dragoon Mountains have some of the most stable winter climbing weather of any rock climbing venue in the United States, but storms can come in at any time. The area is notorious for fierce winds. Summers are hot, but it can be pleasant to climb in the shade even in July. If you do visit between July and September, beware of violent monsoon thunderstorms.

Regulations: All climbs in the Dragoons are on land belonging to the Coronado National Forest. In order to protect nesting peregrine falcons, the Forest Service has instituted an annual closure of the rocks along the divide between the East and West Strongholds. The closure currently runs from March 1–June 30 each year, but contact the Coronado National Forest (520-378-0311) for the latest information. The only areas listed here that are currently subject to these seasonal closures are Cochise Dome and the Rockfellow Group (the climbs *What's My Line* and *Forest Lawn*).

Camping: Beautiful primitive camping exists both at the Isle of You and at the end of the road in the West Stronghold. Several spacious, unregulated sites under the shade of oak and alligator juniper trees are found in both places. No water or services of any kind are available at either camp.

Food and Supplies: The nearest town is Tombstone, a slow 23-mile drive from the Stronghold. This tourist town is well equipped with gas stations and restaurants, but it lacks a grocery store. For groceries go to Sierra Vista, 20 miles beyond Tombstone to the southwest.

Gear: Crack routes at the Stronghold usually require burly racks that include double cams up to a #3 Camalot, and many routes demand even larger cams. Stronghold face routes are protected predominantly via tied-off chickenheads. Bring lots of slings for this purpose, including a number of large (up to 15-foot) slings. Supertape and Spectra slings provide the most snug, secure fit when girth-hitching chickenheads. Figure on bringing around 15 slings in addition to those you would normally use for runners. It is very handy to bring a 55- or 60-meter rope. Get any climbing gear you need in Tucson.

Emergency Services: The nearest medical facilities are at Sierra Vista Regional Health Center, 300 El Camino Real in Sierra Vista , 43 miles and 1 hour of driving from the Stronghold. (520-458-4641)

Kids and Dogs: The Isle of You is perfectly suited for a family excursion. The camping at the Stronghold is beautiful and offers lots of opportunities for hiking, but the long, arduous approaches to the climbs themselves are not very kind to children or short-legged dogs.

Cochise Stronghold West

The climbing at the West Stronghold falls naturally into three distinct geographic areas: the Divide area, the Whale area, and the Warpath Dome area. Each of these areas involves a separate approach that is fairly long and involved. The trails to the Divide and Whale areas depart directly from the camping area in the West Stronghold. The Warpath area is a 3.7-mile drive from the campground.

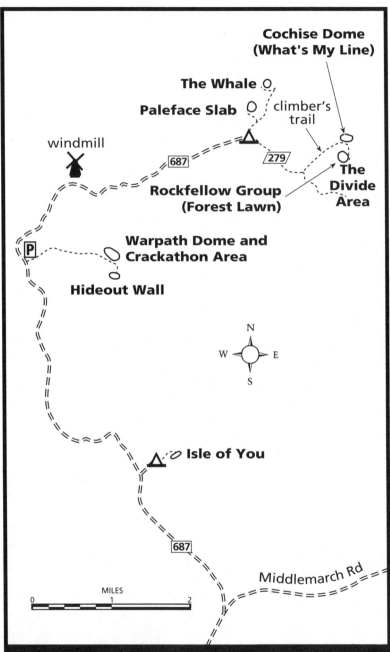

Cochise Dome
(What's My Line)

The Whale

Paleface Slab

climber's
trail

windmill

687

279

Rockfellow Group
(Forest Lawn)

The
Divide
Area

P

Warpath Dome and
Crackathon Area

Hideout Wall

N

W   E

S

Isle of You

687

Middlemarch Rd

MILES

0   1   2

DRAGOON MOUNTAINS CRAGS

THE DIVIDE AREA

The divide that separates the East and West Strongholds bristles with huge granite domes and fins that host the most famous climbs there. Most of these climbs are difficult, strenuous crack climbs, many of them extremely serious. A modest explosion of bolted routes has occurred recently, with little documentation available for many of these routes. Tucked in among some of Arizona's burliest climbs are two more moderate gems.

To approach the Divide from the camping area, hike up Forest Trail 279, which offers a scenic hike from the West Stronghold to the East Stronghold, for about 30 minutes as it ascends through a series of switchbacks and then settles down to a long, fairly level eastward traverse. This traverse ends at a right-hand, hairpin switchback. A faint climber's trail leaves the main trail at this switchback and descends into the wash on the left. Follow this trail to the bottom of the wash, then turn right and ascend the wash. The walking is open and pleasant, with tantalizing views

The crags of the Divide area. Cochise Dome is the prominent sunlit rock just left of center.

of huge towers en route. Cochise Dome (*What's My Line*) is the striking stack of fins to the left, and the Rockfellow Group (*Forest Lawn*) is the cluster of clean, massive domes on the right. After about 15 minutes of walking in the wash you find yourself directly below Cochise Dome, in the narrow gap between it and the Rockfellow Group. Here is where you access *What's My Line*. The approach takes a total of about 45 minutes.

For *Forest Lawn*, continue up the wash past Cochise Dome to the open area of the Divide itself. Cairns mark the trail through here, which passes under a cave formed by a pile of boulders just as it begins to descend the wash on the east side of the pass. About 50 yards beyond this cave a small tributary wash enters from the right (southwest). A cairn usually marks this junction. Ascend this tributary wash and the boulders on its right to the base of the Rockfellow Group, which you reach on their north side. *Forest Lawn* is on Bastion Tower, the farthest tower south in the main group. Turn left when you reach the rocks and traverse along their base until you reach *Forest Lawn*, which is a distinctive left-facing dihedral with neon-green lichen covering its left wall. The total approach time is about 1 hour.

1. WHAT'S MY LINE 5.6 A0 (or 5.10c) ★★★
FA: Dave Baker, Larry Seligman, Peter Depagter 1971

This is Arizona's most famous 5.6, and an unforgettable climb. It tackles the south face of Cochise Dome. The climb is moderate except for one stiff friction move at the very beginning, which most climbers avoid by executing a short, easy pendulum to chickenheads (A0). Because of the pendulum and the almost exclusive use of slung chickenheads for protection, this route isn't the best choice for leaders who are at their limit at 5.6. Consider using a double-rope technique to better protect the second on the pendulum and to minimize rope drag.

Follow the previous approach directions. When you are beneath the south face of Cochise Dome you can see a large ledge that meets the left side of the south face about halfway up. The climb begins where that ledge meets the face. You access the ledge by walking west (backtracking a bit) in the wash until you can easily scramble up to a third-class slot that ends on the ledge. A couple of trees offer landmarks. You will descend on the opposite (northeast) side of the rock, so it is easiest to leave your packs at the point where you leave the wash rather than carting them all the way up to the ledge. Once you are in the third-class slot, continue traversing it right until it ends at the face. A double-bolt anchor marks the beginning of the route.

Pitch One: Climb up and right from the anchor to a bolt. Pendulum right from the bolt to some chickenheads (or face climb directly to the chickenheads at 5.10c). Once you are established on the chickenheads the fun begins! Ascend the continuous line of jugs to a triple-bolt anchor

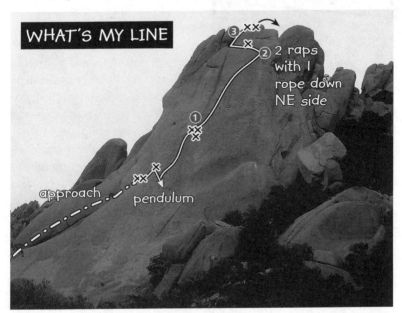

Chance Traub leading the classic dihedral on Forest Lawn

at the base of a prominent brown water streak. If you can't find the bolts amidst all the chickenheads, that's okay because you can set up an excellent belay from chickenheads just about anywhere you choose. 5.5 A0, 150 feet. **Pitch Two:** Continue up the chickenheads, following the path of least resistance, angling right as you go. Climbing doesn't get more fun than this! Set up a belay anchor from chickenheads on the upper right corner of the face. 5.5, 160 feet. **Pitch Three:** Ascend a short headwall and then traverse straight left past a bolt (5.6 crux) to an easy ledge/ramp that leads left to a right-facing dihedral/gully that leads to the top of the dome. 5.6, 100 feet. **Descent:** Do a single-rope rappel northeast from a double-bolt anchor on the summit to a second double-bolt anchor, where another single-rope rappel northeast lands you in the gully north of the rock. Scramble down the gully around the rock's northeast side and around to your packs.

Gear: Bring a modest rack that includes cams, especially in the #½–1 Camalot range, stoppers of all sizes, and lots of slings for tying off the chickenheads that provide most of the protection on the route.

2. FOREST LAWN 5.9 ★★★
FA: Mike McEwen, Gary Axen 1975

Lines don't come any cleaner than the first pitch of this route, which graces the cover of the 1997 edition of *Backcountry Rockclimbing in Southern Arizona*. You can't miss the elegant left-facing dihedral with green lichen covering the left face. The route begins behind a large block. Begin with a step right to access a steep crack. Move left up the crack to the base of the dihedral and then ascend the dihedral to its top. Exit right onto a ledge equipped with a double-bolt anchor. The dihedral is a strenuous lieback that challenges the leader to find creative rest stances. **Descent:** This first pitch is the main event and most parties rappel from the bolts at its top (or do the much harder 5.10c *Pair A Grins* finish). If you want, there is a more moderate optional second pitch, which ascends the 5.7

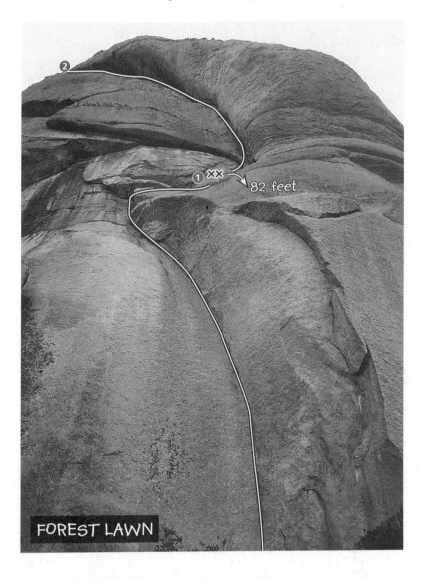

FOREST LAWN

cracks above the belay for 165 feet to a belay stance on chickenheads. From the top of this pitch scramble up to the top of the tower on fourth-class ground and descend a ramp to a double-bolt rappel station. Rappel the chimney to the right (north) of the route using 2 ropes. **Gear:** Bring extra medium cams. **Descent:** You can rappel from pitch 1 with a single 55-meter rope. 110 feet.

THE WHALE AREA

This area encompasses the crags that line the wash north of the campground. Numerous crags host routes here, but this guide lists routes on only two of them. The Paleface Slab, a distinctively white face to the left of the drainage, offers one-pitch friction routes. The Whale is a tall, narrow dome with a wide, left-arching crack near the top that looks like the mouth of a breaching whale. The dome offers long, classic climbs up to five pitches. All of the listed routes on both rocks face south, so they get a lot of winter sun.

The trail to both crags begins from the last parking spot on the left before the circular drive at the road's end. Cairns usually mark the beginning of the trail. The path wanders through the forest for about 200 yards and then goes up the bouldery wash for a short distance before it

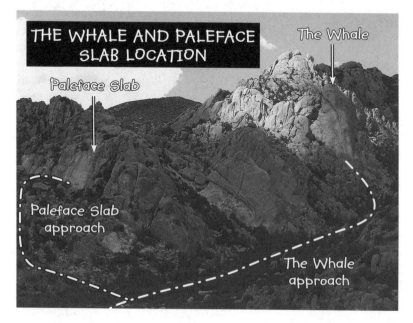

THE WHALE AND PALEFACE SLAB LOCATION

The Whale

Paleface Slab

Paleface Slab approach

The Whale approach

reenters the forest. It emerges from beneath the trees at an open area with good views of the Paleface Slab and the Whale just before it drops back into the wash for the second time, after about 10 minutes of walking. To reach Paleface Slab, clamber up the open slope to the left immediately upon entering the wash for the second time. A cairned route exists here but it is often tricky to spot when you are in the wash itself. It is usually easy to pick it up once you've ascended the slope a short distance. The white rock of Paleface Slab is obvious above you. Aim for the left side of the small pinnacle that lies a good distance down the slope from the Paleface Slab. After passing this pinnacle on the left, the trail continues to angle up and left rather than heading directly to the slab itself. This is to avoid the big boulder pile that lies below the slab. When you reach the same height as Paleface Slab, traverse right past a large pine tree to access the slab's base. The total approach time is about 20 minutes.

For the Whale, continue to follow the main trail where it enters the wash for the second time. Cairns mark the path, which weaves in and out of the wash from this point on. Several trail strands exist, but none of them stray very far from the wash. Continue up the wash until you are directly below the massive south face of the Whale, which takes about 20 minutes. From here turn left and ascend the steep gully that runs up along the south face to the routes. Total approach time is about 40 minutes.

Paleface Slab

1. OJO BLANCO 5.8 ★ Sport
FA: Bob Kerry and Eric Fazio-Rhicard 1989

This route ascends a small rib in the center of the face past 7 bolts, veering right at the top to a double-bolt rappel anchor. The climbing is enjoyable, but the rock is a bit gritty. **Descent:** Rappel the route.

2. PALEFACE 5.9 ★★ Sport
FA: Eric Fazio-Rhicard and Bob Kerry 1989

This is the route on the very clean, white right side of the face. Begin by climbing straight right to a low first bolt from the top of a large boulder at the base of the slab. Continue up a line of 8 bolts to the same anchor as Ojo Blanco. **Descent:** Rappel.

There is a third route on the slab, *Feast of Friends* (5.8), that begins in the water streak left of *Ojo Blanco*. Look for bolts in the water streak. It veers strongly right at the top on runout 5.7 climbing to reach the

Ojo Blanco/Paleface anchor. The rock is poor and the route can't really be recommended.

The Whale

1. MOBY DICK, GRADE III 5.8 ★★★
FA: Bob Kerry and Josh Tofield 1988

This route is a tour de force that offers up five diverse pitches of great face and crack climbing. Don't miss it! Begin at an alcove beneath a set of distinctive, left-leaning cracks that run most of the length of the wall. These cracks lead to the whale's mouth higher up.

Pitch One: Ascend the right crack for 25 feet, then step left and ascend the left crack, which is really a small, left-facing dihedral, past a bolt to a double-bolt belay on a small ledge left of a wide crack. 5.8, 100 feet. **Pitch Two:** Step left to a blunt arête and ascend this. Face climb up and a bit right, just left of the wide crack to a belay ledge with two small trees. 5.7, 100 feet. **Pitch Three:** Continue to face climb up chickenheads to the left of the wide crack/corner, passing a bolt where the corner narrows and steps right. Belay from chickenheads after exhausting your rope. 5.6, 150 feet.

Opposite: The author and Terri Cook climb classic cracks and knobs on Moby Dick. *(Photo: Charlie Crocker)*

Pitch Four: Continue along this crack/corner system 40 feet until you can traverse out of it to the right at a bolt. Continue to face climb up and right past a second bolt and a chimney to a double-bolt belay on a dike below a beautiful face covered with dark brown plates. 5.6, 100 feet. **Pitch Five:** Go straight up the plate-covered face past 2 bolts. It is tougher here to sling chickenheads, as they aren't as incut as those on the lower pitches, but it is possible to get good stoppers and cams in the shallow grooves between some of the plates. The angle of the wall eases off after about 100 feet of climbing, but the best belay stances are to be had from cracks farther up the wall. 5.7+, 165 feet. **Descent:** From here scramble to the top of the dome on fourth-class ground. A triple-bolt rappel anchor equipped with chains facilitates an overhanging double-rope rappel off the west side to the top of the approach gully. Descend this gully to the southeast to return to your packs.

Gear: Bring a light rack that includes stoppers, Aliens, medium cams, and a #3 Camalot, along with abundant tie-off slings for chickenheads.

2. SOUTH FACE, GRADE III 5.7+ R ★★
FA: Kip Metzger

This is an improbable route that ascends the vast south face of the Whale without a crack in sight. There is aesthetic appeal to its no-bolts nature, but it would be a three-star classic if the first-ascent party had chosen to drill just 2 or 3 bolts to shorten the longest runouts. There is a lot of runout climbing, but all of it is on reasonable ground. Given the length of the route and its runouts, it is not recommended for leaders whose limit is 5.7 or for climbers unfamiliar with Stronghold climbing.

This route parallels *Moby Dick* on the right and joins that route for its last pitch. Although the *Moby Dick* cracks are invisible while you are on the route, they are never far away and you can bail off to them at several points. Approach as for *Moby Dick*, but the route begins in an alcove about 50 yards before the *Moby Dick* alcove. A buttress protrudes into the approach gully between this alcove and the start of *Moby Dick*. A red-barked madrone tree stands next to the wall at the beginning of the route. Although you can't see it from the base, the route ascends the face of a flake to the right of the *Moby Dick* cracks.

Pitch One: Ascend the weakness in the wall 10 feet left of the madrone tree to a right-leaning crack. This first 10 feet entails some of the hardest climbing on the route. Move up and right from the crack onto a low-angle ramp, then up to a second, shallow right-leaning crack that offers protection. Step left onto the chickenhead-studded face and ascend it to the top of the flake. A 15-foot sling is needed to lasso the flake for a belay anchor. 5.7, 130 feet. **Pitch Two:** Step down the left side of the pinnacle a short distance to a leftward traverse that leads to a face covered in big chickenheads. Continue up the chickenheads to a 20-foot section of unprotected 5.7 friction climbing, which ends above at more excellent chickenheads. Go straight up the face via large holds to a second friction section that is also runout. The big holds appear again above, taking you to a group of three huge chickenheads that serve as a belay anchor below a steep headwall. This pitch requires a 60-meter rope, as there is no secure belay anchor below the three large chickenheads. 5.7 R, 200 feet. **Pitch Three:** Move straight up for 10 feet to a small ledge that traverses to the right below the headwall. Traverse this ledge for 20 feet to big chickenheads below the headwall—these offer the first protection. Ascend the headwall on monster chickenheads. Continue up the lower angle face above and belay from the highest cluster of large chickenheads. 5.6 R, 130 feet. Alternatively, you can move straight right from the belay to reach the chickenheads below the headwall. This slightly harder option is better protected for the second. **Pitch Four:** Chickenheads continue for about 10 feet above the belay, then end at a long, unprotected friction slab. The holds are positive and the angle is moderate, but the 50-foot

The Dragoon Mountains lie in an especially diverse biotic zone that displays a mixture of Mexican and American species.

runout is definitely an attention getter. Reach chickenheads and good protection above the slab. At a dike that diagonals across the face and has eroded into bulbous chickenheads, move left to a double-bolt belay. This is the belay at the top of *Moby Dick*'s fourth pitch. 5.7 R, 110 feet. **Pitch Five:** Ascend the plate-studded brown face above past 2 bolts for 100 feet to lower-angle rock above. Belay from the first cracks you encounter. This is the final pitch of *Moby Dick*. 5.7+, 165 feet. **Variation:** An alternate start avoids pitch one by climbing the first 20 feet of *Moby Dick* to a small pine tree, where it is possible to step right around the corner to a large bowl. From a belay in the bowl you can reach the belay atop pitch two with a 165-foot rope if you really stretch it out, but a longer rope is still preferable. **Descent:** Same as for *Moby Dick*. **Gear:** Bring a 60-meter rope and a small rack of stoppers, Aliens, and cams to #2 Camalot size. An optional #3 Camalot comes in handy on pitch one. Most of the protection is provided by tied-off chickenheads, so bring lots of slings. Include several 10- and 15-foot-long slings.

THE WARPATH DOME AREA

The Warpath Dome area offers a good concentration of fun one-pitch routes, especially at Hideout Wall, which boasts the best selection of 5.6 routes in the Dragoons. Warpath Dome itself hosts *Warpath*, an excellent long face route, and the Crackathon area on its right flank has several one-pitch crack routes. These climbs are not located in the Stronghold itself but lie on the range's west flank a short drive away.

Bob Kerry's *Backcountry Rockclimbing in Southern Arizona* describes an approach to Warpath Dome that has since been closed due to construction of a private home. Currently, to reach these climbs from the camping area in the West Stronghold, drive Forest Road 687 3.7 miles (0.7 mile beyond the fence and the windmill) to a pullout by a lone oak tree at the crest of a small hill. This is the road's closest approach to Warpath Dome, the largest, most prominent rock in this section of the range. If you are driving directly from Middlemarch Road, drive 9.7 miles on FR 687 to reach the parking area.

A short trail leads northeast, directly toward the house. After 60 yards you will see the fence that encloses the house's private property. You meet the fence near its southwest corner. Turn right and strike out cross-country east, paralleling the fence. When you reach the southeast corner of the fence turn left and follow a ridge that trends north, again parallel to the fence. Drop off the ridge into the wash that truncates it after about 200 yards. A gate is built into the fence where it crosses the wash. Turn right and walk up the wash a short distance to a wide area where two washes converge. Walk up the left (north) wash 30 yards to a trail that climbs steeply out of the wash on its right (looking upstream) side. This is the beginning of a cairn-marked path to the rock. The path crosses open, flat country to the steep gully that passes

Warpath Dome

Crackathon area

Hideout Wall

WARPATH DOME
AND HIDEOUT
WALL LOCATION

approach

below and right of Warpath Dome. You reach the gully after about 15 minutes on the flats. Another 15 minutes of more strenuous walking up the gully brings you level with the start of *Warpath*. To reach *Warpath* continue up the gully a short way until you are slightly above the start of the route and traverse left through a boulder field to the base of the rock. From here descend along the rock to the beginning of the route, which lies just beyond a large, dead tree with a prominent fire scar on it. A live pine whose trunk runs along the ground marks the route's actual beginning.

To reach the Crackathon area, continue up to the end of the gully, which you reach a short distance above the start of *Warpath*. Cairns lead right and slightly downhill for 50 yards as the path breaks into open country again. The Hideout Wall is visible across the head of another gully to the south. The main cairned path heads southeast toward that wall, but here you want to veer left and pick your way up the slope toward the wall with the prominent buttresses separated by wide cracks that form the upper south end of Warpath Dome. You reach the cliff after another 10 minutes, or about 40 minutes total.

For Hideout Wall, continue to follow the cairns toward the southeast after you reach the top of the Warpath Dome gully. The wall is the obvious, low-angle rock cut by clean cracks that lies on the far side of the next gully. The path heads more or less straight for the wall, dropping down into the head of the next gully en route. The total walking time is about 50 minutes.

Warpath Dome

1. WARPATH 5.9- ★★

FA: Karl Rickson, Pat McNerthy, Gene "Smitty" Husted 1975

This climb offers up a strenuous chimney on pitch one and then changes to delightful chickenhead climbing for the next three pitches. Together they add up to a very satisfying climb right up the center of a large and impressive piece of rock. The upper pitches of the route are not obvious at first, but identifying several notable features will help you locate the proper path up the vast face. The first of these features are four parallel dikes that angle down and right across the face. The other important feature is a wide, vertical crack that splits the center of the upper face. The route angles up left along these dikes to reach the wide crack. The route faces southwest.

Pitch One: Tackle the chimney in the prominent right-facing dihedral

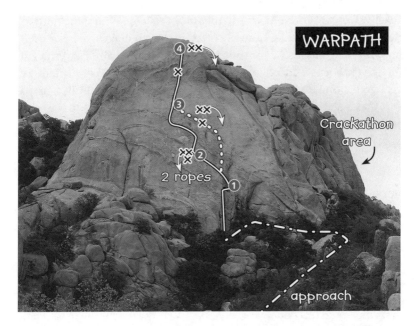

that rises from the left side of the most obvious indentation at the base of the rock, right where the lowest of the four parallel dikes reaches the ground. Where the dihedral ends, traverse right (the route's crux) to a belay ledge at the base of an off-width crack. This pitch uses gear from small Aliens and wired stoppers up through two #3 and one #4 Camalot. 5.9-, 80 feet. **Pitch Two:** Step up and left from the belay onto a dike, the second of the four parallel ones. At this point you have two choices. The standard route, which is easier, follows the dike up and left to a triple-bolt belay (this is the final rappel station for the descent). The alternative, direct route is described after the standard route. 5.6, 60 feet. **Pitch Three:** From the triple-bolt belay go up the face to the next dike (the third of the four) and traverse it left until you reach the base of the wide crack that splits the upper face. Ascend this to a comfortable belay stance in the crack above the fourth dike. 5.7, 100 feet. **Pitch Four:** Continue up the wide crack to its end. Above it lies a vertical dike that splits the steep headwall. Climb the dike on good chickenheads up ever-steepening rock to a rusty bolt. This bolt protects a move left to large chickenheads on a dike that cuts up and right across the face. Heave up over the headwall onto this dike and finish the pitch by either climbing the remainder of the dike up and right or by going straight up the chickenheads on progressively lower-angled rock. Either way leads to a double-bolt belay and rappel station.

5.6, 130 feet **Variation:** An alternative, direct route that combines pitches two and three is possible. From the belay atop pitch one move up and left onto the dike, but instead of continuing left along the dike head straight up a chickenhead-studded face past another dike (the third of the four) to yet another one (the fourth and highest). Traverse left on this dike, past a bolt that is actually part of a 5.10 climb that crosses *Warpath*, to the wide crack mentioned above. Move up this crack to the belay atop pitch three. This route is more difficult than the standard line and is slightly runout, but it is an enjoyable natural line and good protection can be arranged by a careful, deliberate leader. 5.8 R, 140 feet. **Descent:** You can walk off the back side of Warpath Dome and descend southeast to the head of the approach gully, but most people rappel back to the base of the route now that a series of anchors has been established down the face. This descent involves three rappels, the first two of which can be done with one rope, and a third that requires two ropes. The route ends at the first of these anchors. The rappel descends a smoother part of the face, minimizing the danger of stuck ropes. The rappel goes down a 5.10 bolt line that you could easily top-rope. The first rappel ends at a double-bolt anchor, which you use for the second rappel. This second rappel ends at the triple-bolt anchor atop pitch two. From here make a final rappel with 2 ropes to the ground. **Gear:** Aliens through #4, Camalot and tie-off slings for chickenheads.

The Crackathon Area

This is the wall that forms the upper right side of Warpath Dome. A series of chickenhead-covered buttresses are separated from one another by wide cracks. While other routes have been done here, I only describe one. The route faces southwest.

1. DRIVEN BY FEAR 5.8 ★★

FA: Wit Wisniewski, Bob Kerry 1990

The first 10 feet of this climb offer a pure off-width experience that can be avoided by climbing the crack to the right and traversing in above the off-width. The hand crack above is steeper than it looks from below and offers good jamming. Where the crack widens out again the route slides onto the left wall for some steep face climbing up good chickenheads. It finishes at a triple chickenhead belay/rappel anchor just below the top of the buttress. Bring slings to back up the ones that are already there and a knife to cut away some of the really old ones. 110 feet. **Descent:** Rappel the route with 2 ropes. Beware of the rope-eating wide crack.

Hideout Wall

This low-angle wall consists of clean buttresses cleaved by beautiful cracks. It offers the highest concentration of moderate crack routes at the Stronghold and is a wonderful place to hone your crack technique. The routes face northeast. The cairned approach trail drops you off at *We Be Jammin*. *Wide and Forgotten* and *Cruise Corner* are a short distance to the left. To reach *Popeye Crack* drop below some boulders that lie at the base of the wall left of *We Be Jammin* and move left around them. Continue up and left through another boulder pile to the base of the route.

1. POPEYE CRACK 5.8+ ★★
FA: Bob Kerry, Wit Wisniewski 1990

The wall is split by a weakness into left and right halves. This is the most prominent crack that splits the left half. It runs past the left side of a small, rectangular overhang. This is a fun off-width that is not a desperate struggle, making it a great place to practice the technique. The crux is getting to the off-width itself. A series of thin seams leads up to the crack. These moves are easier if you move onto the face to the right of the seams. Adequate protection can be arranged if you bring a #4 RP and some small Aliens. Once you reach the crack, grunt your way up it to a belay station consisting of 1 bolt and a small chickenhead that lies just left of the rectangular roof. **Descent:** Rappel the route using 2 ropes. 130 feet. The off-width protects well if you bring two #3 and two #4 Camalots.

2. WIDE AND FORGOTTEN 5.7 ★

This clean crack splits the lower portion of the face 15 feet left of *Cruise Corner*. It offers 90 feet of fun, independent climbing before it merges with *Cruise Corner*. You will need lots of big cams to protect this pitch. Two #4 and one #5 Camalot will give you peace of mind. The crack starts atop a large boulder perched against the face 15 feet left of *Cruise Corner*. Either ascend the chimney between the block and the wall or do a bouldery, leftward-rising hand traverse to reach the base of the crack. From there the route is obvious. Climb the rapidly widening crack until it turns into a chimney. At that point you can burrow into the chimney, where a smaller crack offers protection, or face climb on positive holds on the outside of the chimney. Cut right at the top of the crack/chimney to join *Cruise Corner*. You need a 55-meter rope to reach the preferred belay atop *We Be Jammin*. Alternatives for those with a 50-meter rope are to either stop at the intermediate belay point described for *Cruise Corner* or begin this route on top of the boulder at the base of the crack. 170 feet. **Descent:** Same as for *We Be Jammin*.

Confident climber cruising Cruise Corner

3. CRUISE CORNER 5.6 ★★
FA: Bob Kerry, Wit Wisniewski 1990

This route ascends the beautiful, right-facing dihedral 40 feet left of *We Be Jammin*. Climb the dihedral via jams and liebacks, then ascend the wide crack above to a chimney. A slung block at the top of the chimney has been used by some parties to rappel, but it is better to carry on to the more redundant rappel anchor at the top of *We Be Jammin*. To reach it, exit the chimney on its right side to a low-angle slab, which you ascend to a narrow ledge with a rap station on a tree above. 165 feet. The route takes gear up to a #3 Camalot, and a #4 Camalot can come in handy for the chimney. **Descent:** Same as for *We Be Jammin*.

4. WE BE JAMMIN 5.7 ★★
FA: Wit Wisniewski, Bob Kerry 1990

The trail deposits you at the base of this fine route, which consists of a hand crack that begins just left of a large boulder that leans against the face. A few face moves lead up seams to the base of the hand crack. Jam the excellent crack to its end. From there either continue up seams directly above or step left to another good crack that continues to a small overlap with a random bolt drilled in it. Move up and left past the bolt to the low-angle face above. Cut right up the face to a tree with rap slings. 140 feet. This tree is backed up by two slung blocks that make for a tangle of slings at the anchor. Bring some extra slings in case you need to leave one for the rappel. **Descent:** Rappel from the tree using two ropes.

Isle of You

The Isle of You offers easily accessible sport climbing that is a complete change of pace from the long cracks and sweeping, chickenhead-protected faces of the Stronghold. It is just off the access road to the West Stronghold, so it makes for a great stop on the way in or out. The climbing occurs on three rocks—Trad Rock, Rad Rock, and Glad Rock—but only Trad Rock has climbs rated 5.10a and below. The climbing involves thoughtful sequences of moves on positive holds, and the climbs are all long, most of them approaching 80 feet and one, *Isle of You* (5.9), ascending 150 feet (requiring 2 ropes to descend). All routes are bolted and each route has its own rappel anchor. The routes are well bolted, but the first ascensionists didn't believe in bolting easy ground. That means there are some runouts.

Trad Rock is the most obvious face you see as you drive the 0.4-mile-long access road off Forest Road 687. Rad Rock lies immediately behind and slightly above it. From the parking area an obvious approach trail crosses the wash and ascends the slope to Trad Rock. The approach takes less than 5 minutes. You reach the face near its right-hand edge, below the water streak that marks *Baby Jr. Gets Spanked*. A clump of oak trees lies to your right, occupying a small platform. To your left is a larger clump of oaks that sits on a much larger platform. These two oak-covered platforms provide useful landmarks for locating the routes.

Most of the routes here were put up in 1993 by the trio of Mike Strassman, Elizabeth Ayers, and Scott Ayers, but routes 6 and 7 are more recent additions with unknown pedigrees.

1. OK CORRAL 5.7 ★★ Sport
This is one of the most enjoyable routes on the crag, a quality moderate amidst a cluster of harder climbs. It ascends the fourth line of bolts from the left edge of the wall. Begin on a small platform formed on top of a pile of boulders that leans against the wall. The route is distinguished by the

presence of 2 bolts very close to the ground. It ascends a brown streak past a small overhang and finishes at an anchor immediately down and right from the only ledge with a small tree on the upper wall. 9 bolts, 80 feet.

2. ISLE OF YOU 5.9 ★★ Sport

This marathon route was the first established on the crag, and it is still one of the best. The route begins on the large, flat platform with the left-hand clump of oak trees on it. The platform's left side is bounded by large boulders, above which rises a prominent left-facing dihedral, the only sizable one on the entire wall. This route tackles the second line of bolts right of that dihedral. It begins immediately left of a lone oak tree that stands very close to the base of the wall. After a frustratingly difficult, bouldery start, the route traverses right past 2 bolts, then heads straight up the wall for 150 feet of great climbing. Short, harder sections are interspersed with comfortable rests, and the holds are positive. It is much easier to belay the second from the top, where the leader can sit in a comfortable divot, than to slingshot this long route. Remember to bring a second rope for the rappel. 14 bolts, 150 feet.

The author leading the marathon pitch of Isle of You *(Photo: Terri Cook)*

3. STONE WOMAN 5.10a ★ Sport

This route shares a start with *Baby Jr.*, and most leaders will want to clip the first bolt on *Baby Jr.* on their way to the high first bolt on *Stone Woman*. If you do that, be sure to use a long sling to avoid rope drag higher on the pitch. Small but positive holds provide passage up this clean face for 80 feet of quality climbing. There is a longish runout between bolts six and seven on fairly easy ground that can be protected if you bring a medium-sized Alien or equivalent piece, but it isn't necessary. 7 bolts (plus the first bolt on *Baby Jr.*), 80 feet.

4. BABY JR. 5.8+ ★ Sport

This is another very good route. It ascends a set of distinctive red overlaps, beginning at the rightmost oak tree of the left group. There are long sections of moderate climbing between the harder bits, and these easier passages don't have bolts, making for some fairly long runouts. There are only 5 bolts in 80 feet of climbing. All of the difficult moves are well protected, though, so the route doesn't feel scary. 5 bolts, 80 feet.

5. BABY JR. GETS SPANKED 5.6 ★★ Sport

This route ascends an obvious, black water streak just left of the right clump of oak trees. The climbing on incut holds is really fun. The first

Puzzling through the sequence on Stone Woman *(Photo: Terri Cook)*

bolt is about 20 feet off the ground because the initial moves are on easy rock just left of a rock bulge. 7 bolts, 85 feet.

6. UNKNOWN 5.9 Sport

There are two recently installed bolt lines to the right of *Baby Jr. Gets Spanked*. This route is the left bolt line of the two. It begins at the same place as *Baby Jr. Gets Spanked* and reaches its first bolt about 20 feet up the wall and 15 feet right of the first bolt on *Baby Jr. Gets Spanked*. The climbing utilizes more rounded, less positive holds than the routes farther left, and the climbing is not as classic as the older routes. It ends at an independent anchor 10 feet right of that for *Baby Jr. Gets Spanked*. It would be quite easy to traverse right from *Baby Jr. Gets Spanked*'s anchors to set up a top rope on this route. 8 bolts, 85 feet.

7. UNKNOWN 5.10a/b Sport

This is the new line of bolts right of route 6. It begins on easy ground but passes through two tricky sections above, with the crux coming just below the anchor. It is not difficult to traverse right from the top anchor of route 6 to the top anchor for this climb if you want to top-rope it. The route is about 100 feet long, so it is safest if you have a 60-meter rope. 10 bolts, 100 feet.

Mount Lemmon

Mount Lemmon is one of the most famous climbing venues in Arizona. The Mount Lemmon Highway winds 27 miles from the 2500-foot-high desert basin that hosts Tucson to the 9157-foot-high summit of the Santa Catalina Mountains. Known as one of Arizona's "sky islands," the Catalinas' cooler, upper slopes host high-elevation biotic communities that cannot migrate across the hot desert, thus forming "islands." Traveling from base to peak on Mount Lemmon, the dramatic elevation gain takes you through seven distinct life zones, offering equivalent biologic diversity to that encountered on a trip from Mexico to Canada! Impressive rock formations hosting over 1500 climbs are scattered along the highway nearly from base to summit. This wide range of climbing elevations makes Mount Lemmon a premier year-round destination.

The climbing at Mount Lemmon is so close to Tucson that all of the gear shops, restaurants, nightlife, and other amenities you could possibly want are within easy reach. Comfortable campgrounds are located just a short drive from the crags, or you could easily commute from a Tucson hotel without sacrificing climbing time. This is urban climbing at its very best!

The highest concentration of quality moderate climbs is located at Windy Point, 14 miles up the mountain from Tucson. Many ribs of steep, solid granite-gneiss rock

Chance Traub on the Ridgeline classic
Glowing in the Distance

are poised above a deep valley, offering breathtaking views of Tucson as well as hundreds of high-quality, one- and two-pitch routes. This unusual, banded rock resembles granite, but it has some distinct differences. Square-cut face holds abound, and most routes link discontinuous cracks via steep sections of face climbing. A few sport climbs exist here, but most routes involve a mixture of bolt clipping and gear placements. At 6500 feet and with climbs facing in all directions, Windy Point has a moderate climate that lends itself to year-round climbing. Some of the crags are literally steps away from the car, while others, though only a steep 5-minute walk from the road, are insulated from its fumes, noise, and commotion.

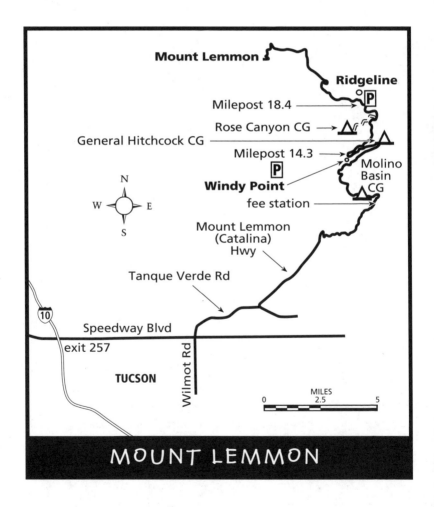

MOUNT LEMMON

Farther up the mountain, at 7300 feet, the Ridgeline crag is a moderate climber's paradise. Ten outstanding sport climbs, none harder than 5.10a, grace its compact face. You can set up shop at the base of the crag and tick off one quality climb after another without moving your pack. The crag is an easy 15-minute walk from your car across rolling, ponderosa pine–clad slopes, and it has a peaceful ambiance that is an enjoyable change of pace from the steep, airy, bustling feel of Windy Point. The rock here is more granite than gneiss, with positive holds allowing surprisingly reasonable passage over bulging rock.

If you exhaust the climbs in this book, there are many other quality crags on Mount Lemmon to keep you occupied for weeks on end. Some of the better choices for a high concentration of moderate climbs include the Beaver Wall/North Fin area at Windy Point, Gumby Wall, Green Slabs, and Chimney Rock. Eric Fazio-Rhicard's comprehensive guidebook *Squeezing the Lemmon II* has all the information you need to enjoy these routes.

MOUNT LEMMON BETA

Drive time from Tucson ▲ 30–45 minutes
Drive time from Phoenix ▲ 2 hours
Drive time from Flagstaff ▲ 4 hours

Getting there: From I-10, take the Speedway exit (exit 257) and drive east through Tucson on Speedway to Wilmot Road. Turn left (north) and follow Wilmot until it changes to Tanque Verde at a right-bending curve. About 4 miles after turning off Speedway, turn left at a sign for the Catalina Highway (synonymous with the Mount Lemmon Highway). For Windy Point, proceed up the winding, mountain road 14.3 miles to a large parking area on a hairpin turn (the Windy Point scenic overlook). For Ridgeline, continue up the road to milepost 18.4 and park on the wide shoulder below the obvious landslide scar. Sollers Point Road comes in from the left at the uphill side of this scar. The highway is a fee demonstration project of the U.S. Forest Service, so there is a charge to use the road. At the time of publication, a day-use pass cost $5, and a weekly pass was $10. A fee collection station is located along the highway just below the Molino Basin Campground.

Approach: See the individual area sections for approach information. The approaches take 2–15 minutes at Windy Point and 15 minutes at Ridgeline.

Season and Elevation: Because of the potential to climb at a variety of elevations and given the different orientations of the climbs, this is a year-round climbing destination. Windy Point regularly lives up to its name and can be very chilly in the winter. Summers are hot but not unreasonable, especially in the shade. Ridgeline offers cooler temperatures due to its higher elevation, but since all climbs there face south, they can provide pleasant winter warmth and, conversely, can be uncomfortably hot in the summer. The best weather occurs in fall and spring. Beware of electrical activity during the localized, heavy thunderstorms from July through September.

Regulations: All of the climbs are on Coronado National Forest land. There are seasonal raptor nesting closures, generally from February through July, but they do not currently affect the areas outlined in this guide. Check with the Forest Service for the most up-to-date closure information.

Camping: There are six Forest Service campgrounds along the Mount Lemmon Highway. Molino Basin, at 4400 feet, is the lowest and therefore warmest. It is closed during the summer. General Hitchcock, at 6000 feet, is open year-round and provides the easiest access to Windy Point, but it was temporarily closed as of the publication date of this book because of damage caused by the 2003 fire. Neither of these campgrounds has water. Rose Canyon campground, at 7000 feet, is very close to the climbs at Ridgeline and is also reasonably convenient to Windy Point. It is usually open from mid-April through late October. It does have water when it is open.

Food and Supplies: Tucson can appease your palate for everything from a convenient grocery store to abundant, inexpensive Mexican restaurants and other international cuisine.

Gear: A standard rack with a set of RPs will suffice on most climbs. An extra set of camming devices and small tri-cams can be helpful on some routes. A single 50-meter rope is sufficient for all routes except where noted in the climb descriptions. Many of the longer routes wander, so clipping some of your gear placements with long slings makes rope management easier.

Emergency Services: The closest hospital to the crags is Tucson Medical Center at 5301 Grant Road. (520-327-5461)

Kids and Dogs: Given the proximity of Tucson and the abundance of noteworthy nearby attractions (e.g., Saguaro National Park, the Arizona-Sonora Desert Museum, and Old Tucson), there is plenty to do on rest days and to keep the nonclimbers in your party occupied while you play. Ridgeline has an easy approach that is kid- and dog-friendly, but the steep, loose approaches to Windy Point climbs (except for Hitchcock Pinnacle and Practice Rock) don't lend themselves well to little legs.

Windy Point

All of the routes described here are on the crags at or east of the main Windy Point parking lot at milepost 14.3. The Windy Point area was hit hard by the huge forest fire of 2003, when most of the area's vegetation

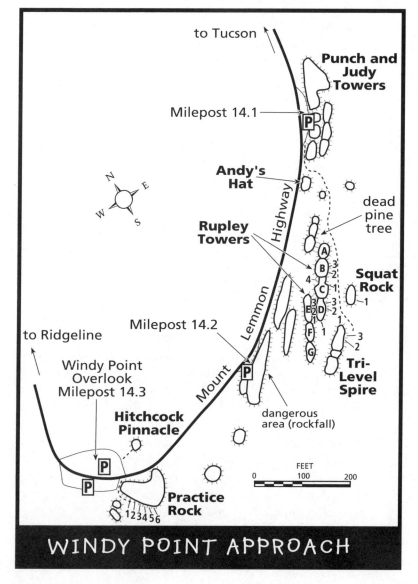

WINDY POINT APPROACH

was torched. As of the time of writing, that lack of vegetation has made navigating the area easier than in the past, but annoying, weedy plants are already starting to take hold.

A recent highway improvement project was conducted with little regard for the beauty and the recreational value of the slopes below the highway. Workers trundled massive boulders down the steep slopes, turning once-steep but reasonable descent gullies into bowling alley death traps. Bouncing boulders sheared off bolts at Indigo Tower and partially buried the climbs on New Wave Wall. The shocking devastation has rendered several popular climbing walls completely unsafe to access or to climb. Fortunately, the walls listed here were not affected by this wanton destruction, and you can climb safely here, out of striking range of the precariously perched granite missiles that the road crews left balanced above other walls. If your climbing plans take you to the Wind Wall, Indigo Tower, Pullout Wall, Stovepipe, or Microwave Wall, check with the local climbing shops about current closures and conditions.

These routes are extremely popular and can be crowded on weekends.

HITCHCOCK PINNACLE

This is the tower immediately uphill from the main Windy Point parking area. It can be accessed by walking east about 1 minute to the base.

1. HITCHCOCK 5.7 or 5.8 ★

This 40-foot-tall spire makes for some very photogenic climbing. The hordes of tourists will be amazed at your spiderlike prowess! Begin on the north side of the pinnacle and worm your way up an easy chimney to the top of a short block just right (west) of the pinnacle. Move up the spire's west face, clipping a bolt that is just out of reach when you are standing on the top of the block. Two variations are possible after clipping the bolt. The easier (5.7) option moves left onto the spire's north face and up to the top. There used to be a second bolt to protect this section, but it has been chopped. Horizontal cracks offer protection in lieu of the bolt. A better-protected and more enjoyable alternative (5.8) tackles the obvious hand crack above the bolt at the junction of the north and west faces. Move left at the crack's end to finish on surprisingly well-protected, exciting face climbing on the north face. **Descent:** Rappel off the spire's north face from bolts. Camming devices (from tiny Aliens to medium Camalots) will get you up the climb.

Climbing Hitchcock Pinnacle is a real crowd-pleaser.

PRACTICE ROCK

This is where Tucson learns to climb. This 40-foot-high rock is so perfectly set up for teaching a beginner to climb that it is hard to believe it wasn't constructed by climbers. If you want to get a lot of climbing done in a short period of time and get acquainted with Mount Lemmon rock, this is your crag. All of the routes here are top-roped. The cliff lies directly below the road at the main Windy Point parking area. The top of the crag lies directly below the wrought-iron fence surrounding the Windy Point overlook. A one-minute stroll from the parking lot puts you at the top of the rock, where you will see six sets of top-rope bolts. Bring some long slings to ensure that your rope isn't rubbing over the edge during the climbing. A 2-minute walk around the west side of the rock places you at the base. The only drawback to the climbing here is that the rock's base is so close to the road that it is a popular party spot. Look out for trash and occasional broken glass here. You can wander nearly at will on the textured face, and none of the climbs are named. The listings below indicate the difficulty level you can expect when climbing the most natural line from each set of anchors.

Since these climbs were viewed as practice routes, nobody kept first ascent records for them.

1. UNNAMED 5.8 ★

The first 15 feet provide some thoughtful moves up small cracks before yielding to easy rock above.

2. UNNAMED 5.5 ★

This route is a good first choice for beginners, as it provides big holds up the textured wall.

3. UNNAMED 5.6 ★

The wall here is a bit steeper than it is to the left or the right, making for slightly more challenging climbing.

HITCHCOCK PINNACLE AND PRACTICE ROCK

Climber silhouetted against the big southern Arizona sky on No Mystique

4. UNNAMED 5.5 ★

More fun climbing up a wall that looks more difficult from below than it really is.

5. UNNAMED 5.6 ★

A bit steeper and longer than routes to the left.

6. UNNAMED 5.7 ★

This is the longest and steepest of the routes on Practice Rock. It looks quite difficult from below, but great holds make for reasonable and fun climbing.

RUPLEY TOWERS

These towers provide some of the longest, as well as some of the best, climbs at Windy Point. Seven separate towers crown a double fin of steep, solid rock. The towers are labeled A through G. The towers possess a greater concentration of moderate grade routes than any other Windy Point crag. They are situated below the highway, about 0.1 mile east (down the road) from the main parking area. Two small parking areas lie downcanyon from the main parking lot, the first at milepost 14.2 and the second at milepost 14.1. Prior to the 2004 road construction, the Towers were accessed from a trail that descended directly below the parking area at milepost 14.2, but the havoc that the construction crews wrought on this area makes access from here much more difficult as well as quite dangerous due to the many giant, loose rocks they have left poised above the approach gullies.

Although it increases the approach time by a couple of minutes, it is now far better to approach the Towers from the pullout at milepost 14.1. This small pullout is distinguished by a group of several towers that rise just off the road (these are the uphill edges of the Punch and Judy Towers). One squat tower (Andy's Hat) lies apart from the others a short distance up the road. Clamber over the retaining wall between Andy's Hat and the other towers and cautiously descend the steep slope below. The first 50 feet are very steep and loose, but the angle lessens and the footing improves immediately below. Continue southwest down the gully and pass left of an impressive spire. From here you can see the taller, downslope faces of the Punch and Judy Towers off to your left. Hang a right here and make a descending traverse below a long, high rock wall, which is the Big Pine Tower massif. The Rupley Towers are the set of rocks ahead and immediately down the slope from the Big Pine Towers. A tall, dead ponderosa pine stands at the entrance to a narrow corridor that separates the Big Pine Towers from the Rupley Towers. To reach the climbs on Tower E, pass this tree and continue through the corridor behind Towers C and D. The descents from all the towers utilize this corridor. To reach Towers A through D, continue your traverse and scramble around the northeast edge of the Rupley massif. The towers are separated from one another by steep, narrow gullies that don't quite reach the ground. As you pass beneath the massif's southeast face you encounter the towers in order from A to D. An open, rolling slope at the base of the cliff provides a nice staging area for all these climbs.

The approach to the towers takes about 10 minutes. The routes all face southeast, with the Tower A through D routes getting lots of sunshine. The Tower E routes start in the narrow, shady corridor between the two ribs of rock that form the Rupley Towers, so they are a great choice for hot days.

Rupley Towers B and C
Descend from each of these towers via a short rappel off the back (northwest) side into the corridor mentioned in the approach information.

Walk right (northeast) along the corridor to the dead ponderosa then turn right to return to the base of the climbs.

1. R-3 5.8 ★★
FA: John Rupley 1960s

This route provides a beautiful, two-pitch traverse of Tower C. **Pitch One:** Begin in a gully on the extreme right side of Tower C. Scramble up and left in the gully to a bolt at its top. Four more bolts show the way and provide protection for the left-angling traverse up the wonderfully textured rock above. Stoppers and cams then protect the remainder of the traverse to a comfortable ledge on the left side of the rock. Two bolts provide an anchor here. 5.8, 90 feet. **Pitch Two:** Step up and into a left-facing, flaky corner. Ascend this and the low-angle face above to a right-facing dihedral. Pass a bolt at the top of this dihedral and step right to a wide crack that can be ascended via fun face climbing on its right-hand wall. Top out on a shoulder of the buttress and then step left to scamper up a short face to a bolt anchor on the true summit. 5.7, 80 feet. The belay anchor at the top of pitch one makes a perfect top-rope anchor for the first pitch of *Bop Till You Drop*, a fun, 5.10a face climb marked by 3 bolts on the lower wall.

2. R-1 5.8+ ★★★
FA: John Rupley 1960s

This is a spectacular, classic, two-pitch route up the elegant face of Tower B. **Pitch One:** Begin beneath a short flake on the left side of Tower B. Ascend the flake 10 feet and then step 10 feet right to a left-facing dihedral. Pass a bolt and continue up a left-angling, blocky corner. Move right at the top of the corner to a double-bolt belay on a ledge. 5.8, 90 feet. **Pitch Two:** Stem up the corner with the wide crack in it directly above the belay, passing a couple of roofs. A beautiful, thin crack that splits the steep face above offers some of the most beautiful climbing at Mount Lemmon. Ascend this crack to the tower's summit. 5.8+, 90 feet. This climb swallows a selection of gear from stoppers and Aliens to large cams.

3. SHEER ENERGY 5.9 ★
FA: Steve Grossman, Dave Baker 1979

This is a fun route that tackles Tower B in one long pitch. Begin in the center of Tower B's southeast face, below a prominent crack. Face climb

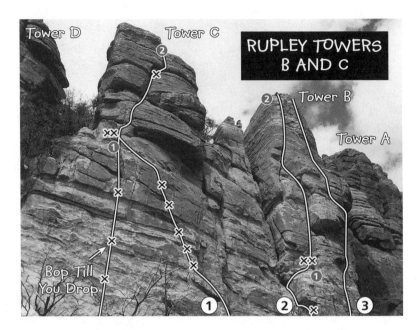

up to the crack and ascend it to a short, rightward-trending section of face climbing to reach a right-facing corner. Ascend the corner to its capping roof. Turn the roof on the left and up a short slab to another crack. Face climb above the end of the crack to the summit. Bring a generous rack for this 140-foot pitch.

Rupley Tower D

Descend into the corridor on the back side of the tower via a dramatic, single-rope rappel. The rappel anchors are situated on the back side of the highest block of rock on the tower, so they are not immediately obvious upon reaching the top.

1. TROUBLE IN PARADISE 5.9 ★★
FA: Mike Strassman, Scott Ayers 1990

This is an exciting and photogenic climb up the left skyline arête of Tower D. It begins at a double-bolt belay anchor next to a small, dead tree halfway up the buttress. You can reach the start either by scampering up the low-angle slab that lies below the buttress-bounding gully or by descending the short gully from the start of the Tower E climbs. From the bottom belay anchor, work up a series of overlaps past 2 bolts, taking advantage of some great holds to heave yourself up the slightly overhanging rock.

Stoppers and small cams protect easier but exposed rock above to a third bolt. The angle kicks back considerably above that bolt until you reach the base of a small, steep corner near the top. A fourth bolt protects a tricky move up this corner. 80 feet.

2. R-4 5.9 ★★★
FA: John Rupley 1960s

Another Rupley Towers classic! It is a long, sustained pitch. Begin near the right side of Tower D, at an arching ramp that begins just off the ground. Either traverse the left side of the arching ramp to a bolt immediately above it or tackle the steep, bouldery face directly below the bolt (this latter option entails a 5.10 move). Move up the face past the bolt to a left-leaning crack that takes you around an overhang to

Trouble in Paradise *provides plenty of exposure.*

the ledge immediately above. Move up the face above the ledge and angle left along a series of flakes, aiming for the beautiful hand crack that splits the prominent roof. Turn the roof and run up the fabulous crack above to the summit. 150 feet. A generous rack containing stoppers through medium cams is in order.

3. LOST RUPLEY ROUTE 5.7 ★
FA: Unknown, but probably John Rupley 1960s

There is some loose rock on this route, but it is an enjoyable meander up the right side of Tower D. Begin at the arching ramp described for R-4. Clip the bolt above the ramp and move up the face and into the left-leaning crack leading through the overhang and up to the ledge described for that climb. From the ledge, trend right and up the face to a boxy seam. A good gear placement exists here to protect you as you move up the runout, low-angle face above to a prominent V-slot up and right. From the top of the V-slot ascend easy (5.4) but loose and poorly

protected rock to the top. There are several old, rusty bolts and a fixed pin on the upper part of the route. None of these fixed pieces is very reliable, and you should back them up with gear placements. A #3 and #4 Camalot are useful, and long slings reduce rope drag. Bring a 60-meter rope.

Rupley Tower E

These climbs are tucked into a narrow corridor behind Tower D. They are short but fun and are less committing than the longer routes on the other towers. They are located a short distance to the left from the end of the Tower D rappel, so you can easily tick them off on your way down from one of those routes. They offer a great respite from the heat due to the shade cast on them all morning from Tower D, which is situated to the east. All of these routes have double-bolt top anchors for the rappel.

RUPLEY TOWER E

1. OBE WAN KANOBEE 5.6 ★

FA: Ben Burnham 2000

The corridor between Towers D and E ends at a rock wall with a hole big enough to crawl through at the base. A chimney slashes Tower E right at this blockage. This climb ascends the low-angle arête that forms the chimney's right side. Two bolts protect the lower portion of the arête; small stoppers and cams provide protection up to a third bolt. The finish is easy above the third bolt, but it is runout and on grainy rock. Rappel from the bolted top anchor. 70 feet.

2. R-2 D-2 5.6 ★

FA: Jay Ladin, Mike Strassman 1983

This climb ascends the right-angling jam crack 10 feet right of *Obe Wan Kanobee*. It begins as a chimney/groove before settling down into some nice hand jams. The crux is found where the hand crack peters out for about 10 feet. The protection in this section is adequate but not abundant. Cracks and flakes continue on the right just past this stretch and continue to the double-bolt rappel anchor. 70 feet. **Gear:** From small wires to a #4 Camalot.

3. R-SENIO 5.7 R ★

FA: Scott Ayers 1991

This used to be an X-rated death climb, but someone has recently added 3 bolts that make the climb much safer. Alternatively, you can easily reach the independent top anchors for this climb from the top of *R-2 D-2* to top-rope it. The climbing is enjoyable, the best on this face. The climb begins 10 feet right of *R-2 D-2* at an eyebolt bottom anchor. Move up the slab to a bolt, then up ledges to a second bolt on a bulge. Use caution clipping the second bolt to avoid a possible ground fall. From here move up easier rock, using wires and small cams, to a top rappel anchor. 70 feet.

4. OUT ON BAIL 5.10a Sport ★★

FA: Mike Argueso, Tony Lusk, Yantz Cox 1990

This fun, pumpy climb is not actually located on Tower E, but rather on the back side of Tower C. It is listed with the Tower E climbs because it is accessed from the same corridor used for their approach. As you hike southwest along the corridor from the dead ponderosa, you see on your left a prominent slot separating Towers B and C. *Out On Bail* climbs the clean, north-facing slab on the right side of this slot. Scramble 15 feet down to a flat staging area in the slot at the base of the climb. Traverse in from the right on a narrow ledge to the first bolt. Shuffle left to a prominent flake and lieback past a second bolt to lower-angled rock above. This lieback is great fun, but it can easily sap your strength, leaving you powerless for the tricky crux moves at the top. Pass a third bolt to a flake that offers the last semblance of a rest. Clip a fourth bolt above and move up and left to the chain anchor at the top. Only quickdraws are required on this sport route. 40 feet.

OUT ON BAIL

Tri-Level Spire

This eye-catching spire lies 50 feet down the hill from Rupley Tower D. Approach it just as you would the Rupley Towers. The rappel descent from *No Mystique* is described with the climb. The other climbs are descended by walking off to the right on a spacious ledge. This ledge provides easy access for top-roping these challenging climbs.

TRI-LEVEL SPIRE
(No Mystique)

80 feet

x-x

1

1. NO MYSTIQUE 5.6 ★

This climb up the narrow north face of the spire looks intimidating from a distance and provides for some great hero photo ops! The north face is split by an obvious series of cracks. Cracks on the right lead up to a stance below the main crack. Fun jamming takes you up this main crack to an easy chimney finish and an obvious belay ledge. This isn't the top of the spire, but it is the top of the route. Bring a long sling for the belay anchor. Desend from double bolts that form the top anchor for *Domestique* (5.11). It is awkward to reach down to these bolts and begin the rappel, so exercise caution. If you are up for a challenge, you can easily top-rope *Domestique*. 80 feet.

Kate McEwen jams the upper crack on No Mystique.

2. DR. SNIFF AND THE TUNA BOATERS 5.10a ★★ Sport

FA: Mike Argueso, Jim Mullins 1990

This is a fun sport route on the lower east face of Tri-Level Spire, below a prominent ledge that provides great top-rope access to this and *Paul and Peggy's Route*. To reach this and the next climb, descend the slope east of *No Mystique* for 150 yards to the base of the wall. *Dr. Sniff* is in the middle of the face, at the right edge of a left-angling overhang that crosses the lower portion of the rock. Six bolts lead up the clean, elegant face above the overhang. Reach the first bolt either by a frontal assault over the overhang or traverse in from the right. In either case, use a spotter. From there, dance up the face past the bolts to the double-bolt top anchor. Traverse off right along the ledge. 6 bolts. 60 feet.

3. PAUL AND PEGGY'S ROUTE 5.9 R or 5.9 TR ★

FA: Paul Davidson, Peggy Davidson 1990

This is a tricky and scary lead, but it makes a great top rope. Begin at the same place as *Dr. Sniff*, but move up the right-angling seams. A bolt is

located at the top of the series of seams. Finish by climbing up past another bolt in the face of the steep block immediately below the ledge. If you do decide to lead this route, bring lots of RPs, stoppers, and Aliens. 60 feet.

Squat Rock
Squat Rock is located 70 feet downhill from Rupley Tower C. Its top forms the "squat" rock that lies below that tower. You can easily walk off the

top here. To approach the rock, descend the gully to either side of this outcrop, a 2-minute walk from Rupley Tower C.

1. ASLEEP AT THE WHEEL 5.9+ ★★
FA: Peter Noebels, John Steiger 1981

You can't miss this beautiful crack! It angles up and right across the smooth southeast face of the rock. Bring a good selection of small to medium-sized cams. 40 feet.

Ridgeline

This cliff is just what the doctor ordered for a fun, relaxing day of climbing at a moderate grade. It hosts ten really enjoyable sport routes on clean, textured rock in a beautiful pine forest. The southern exposure, high elevation, and dappled shade along the base make this a great place for anything from warm climbing on a crisp winter day to comfortable climbing in the

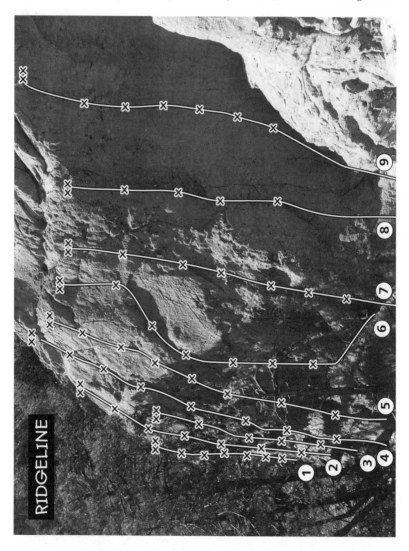

heat of summer. You can set up shop here and tick every route without ever moving your pack. A 50-meter rope and a rack of quickdraws is all you'll need. The crag can get quite crowded on the weekends.

From the parking area, walk up the road (left) to the edge of the landslide scar. Ascend a tiny, rocky drainage on the left side of the scar. The trail is obscure for the first 30 feet as it ascends the steep rubble of the road cut, but it becomes obvious immediately above. Follow the trail up the drainage until it peters out in a gentle swale at the crest of a ridge. Turn left (west) onto a faint trail just below the actual ridgeline crest. The trail is usually marked by a cairn. If you miss the cairn and reach the crest, just turn left and walk along the forested ridgeline. There are beautiful views east into the San Pedro River valley. A cluster of rocks is obvious to the west where the nearly flat ridge becomes steep again. Ridgeline is the cleanest-looking of these crags. Where the trail passes off the level ridge crest and onto the west slopes of the next hill, it forks. Take the right fork, which leads to the base of Ridgeline after about 60 yards of level walking. The approach takes about 15 minutes. Each climb here has its own rappel anchor.

1. SMALL BROWN MOUSE 5.9 ★ Sport
FA: Robert Fleugher, Elaine Flaugher 1994
This route, the leftmost line of bolts on the face, entails sequency climbing up bulging rock. 6 bolts. 70 feet.

2. SISSYBOYZ-8 5.8 ★★ Sport
FA: Robert Fleugher, Tom Weaver 1994
Pulling the crux roof on big jugs is great fun! This is the second bolt line from the left, between two big ponderosa pines. 6 bolts. 70 feet.

3. FIRE ZONE 5.8+ or 5.10a ★ Sport
FA: Tony Lusk, Marti Woerner 1993
The 5.10a crux of this route is a bouldery move right off the ground that can be easily avoided. It is the third line of bolts from the left. Good holds take you over a roof below the fourth bolt. 4 bolts. 50 feet.

4. SUDDEN IMPACT 5.8 ★ Sport
FA: Tony Lusk, Pat Gilbreath 1993
The climbing on this fourth bolt line from the left is very moderate except for a tricky start and a juggy bulge at the fourth bolt. 7 bolts. 80 feet.

5. NEVER TO BE THE SAME 5.8 ★★ Sport
FA: Tony Lusk, Mike Witt 1993

This fifth bolt line from the left has lots of nice climbing. As with many of these routes, the bulge provides the crux, which feels like swinging on the monkey bars at recess during elementary school. 7 bolts. 80 feet.

6. WIND OF CHANGE 5.7 ★★ Sport
FA: Tony Lusk, Mike Witt 1993

This route (the sixth bolt line from the left) provides quality climbing without a bulge to pull over. The crux consists of delicate, slabby moves with thin edges as you move past the last bolt. You can approach the first bolt directly from below or traverse in from a ledge on the right, which is shared with *Two Birds with One Stone*. 6 bolts. 75 feet.

7. TWO BIRDS WITH ONE STONE 5.7 ★★ Sport
FA: Tony Lusk, Kent Brewner   1993

This is the seventh bolt line from the left side of the wall. It starts behind a solitary, dead ponderosa pine. Move up to the ledge and continue up the line of bolts above its right side. The climbing here utilizes good edges up the clean face. 6 bolts. 70 feet.

8. MOGENHEAD 5.8 Sport
FA: Robert Fleugher 1994

Although this is the least aesthetic climb on the wall, it is still worth doing. It is the eighth line of bolts from the left. The route has only 4 bolts in 70 feet and could probably use one more, but the runouts aren't too bad. Be careful clipping the second bolt to avoid the potential ground fall. The climbing is significantly easier if you slide right, onto a series of low-angle ramps. 4 bolts. 70 feet.

9. GLOWING IN THE DISTANCE 5.9 ★★★ Sport
FA: Tony Lusk, Kent Brewner 1993

This is the premier route at Ridgeline. It is the rightmost line of bolts. The climb begins on a slabby face next to a gully that marks the right edge of Ridgeline. The climbing steepens above the first bolt to provide wonderful climbing up a green-tinged wall with spectacular views of the

Opposite: Chance Traub gets Two Birds with One Stone.

San Pedro River valley off to the right. The holds are very positive, but the climbing is less juggy and more sequency than most of the routes on the cliff. 6 bolts. 75 feet.

10. RIDGEBACK 5.5 ★★★ Sport
FA: Kevin Carmichael, Tim Lee 1995

This is a wonderful route for beginning leaders, and the views are spectacular! It occupies the next rib of rock down and east of the main Ridgeline rock. To reach it, walk down the gully at the base of *Glowing in the Distance* until you can round the corner to the left (east) below the next buttress. *Ridgeback* tackles the left arête of this buttress. 7 bolts. 100 feet. **Descent:** Rappel 50 feet west (toward the main Ridgeline cliff) from bolts on the summit.

Tim Yuen styles up the sequential moves of Glowing in the Distance.

RIDGEBACK

50 feet

Main Ridgeline Rock

10

Queen Creek

Queen Creek is the premier sport climbing area in Arizona and one of the closest climbing venues to Phoenix. It is also one of Arizona's largest climbing areas, with hundreds of climbs as well as world-famous bouldering at numerous subareas sprawled over several square miles.

The climbing is on welded tuff, a volcanic rock known for its steep, pocketed faces adorned with tiny crimping edges. Cracks are less abundant and often crumbly, but a few Queen Creek cracks are worthwhile. The rock, known as the Apache Leap tuff, was erupted explosively from a gigantic caldera volcano about 20 million years ago. Later erosion broke apart the once continuous sheet of rock into the maze of spires and buttresses that litter the landscape today. The many pockets and horizontal seams that make welcome climbing holds formed as gas pockets and chunks of soft pumice were flattened by the weight of overlying material. The pumice chunks are more easily eroded than the surrounding rock, causing them to be excavated to form the abundant pockets that so attract climbers here. The tuff is exceptionally abrasive, and your fingers will let you know it after a hard day of pocket pulling.

The highest concentration of moderate routes is located at the Mine area. Rising from a pleasant oak woodland covered with wildflowers during spring, numerous small spires provide steep, pocketed face climbs up to a half pitch in length. This is a particularly

Climber on Snorkeling in the Rhyolite

good family climbing venue because of the easy approaches and short pitches, some of which can be set up as top ropes. Unfortunately, the Mine area is also the most threatened climbing area in Arizona. Lying 7000 feet underground beneath the welded tuff are older granites that contain the richest copper deposit remaining in the United States. Resolution Copper Company, an international conglomerate, wants to mine this lode, the mineral rights to which it already owns. The surface land is public land, managed by the Tonto National Forest. Because Resolution wants to employ a mining technique that would cause the land to sink, it proposed to buy from the U.S. Forest Service surface rights to 760 acres of land above the ore body. In exchange, it offered 4800 acres of private land throughout Arizona that they consider to have outstanding values comparable to those of Queen Creek. Due to opposition from environmentalists and climbers, the land swap deal languished in Congress, causing Resolution to modify the offer. It is now proposing to buy even more land around Oak Flat—3025 acres—in exchange for 5500 acres elsewhere, including land for a climbing-focused state park at Tam-O-Shanter Peak, south of Oak Flat. As this book went to press, the land swap deal was still pending in Congress.

If the land swap goes through, the land will be closed to all recreation, not just climbing. The popular Oak Flat Campground will be closed and prime hiking terrain and Native American acorn gathering areas will be lost. Queen Creek climbing will be hit particularly hard. The venue for the annual Phoenix Boulder Blast, the world's largest bouldering competition, will be taken away. Not only will the area's best concentration of moderate climbs be permanently closed (and when mining starts, destroyed as the land collapses into the hole), but access to the plethora of excellent climbs in Devil's Canyon, including the second-biggest concentration of moderate routes at Queen Creek, will be cut off.

For the land swap to occur, congressional legislation is required. Members of Arizona's congressional delegation have drafted a bill to facilitate the swap, a bill that is now pending in both chambers. Many groups support the swap because of the high-paying jobs the mine will bring to Superior, the mining community nearby that has fallen on hard times since the last mine in the area closed years ago. Even some environmental groups support the legislation because of the high value they place on the lands Resolution is offering in exchange. Other groups, such as the Sierra Club and the Maricopa County Audubon Society, oppose the plan because the land swap would allow the company to sidestep the rigorous environmental assessment that is required for any mining project on public lands. They also find troubling the fact that this bill would be a complete reversal from the special protection that President Dwight Eisenhower accorded this land in 1955 when he withdrew the area from mining activity in order to preserve its outstanding scenic attributes and recreational opportunities.

Congressional action on land swaps often takes years, though if enough political momentum builds it can happen in the twinkling of an eye. The actual mining will not begin for fifteen years in any event, as there is much exploratory and engineering work that must be done. There is still time to make your voice heard on this issue. If you want to find out more, check out the current status, or add your voice to those trying to preserve public access to this beautiful climbing venue, visit the Friends of Queen Creek website (*www.friendsofqueencreek.com*) or contact the Access Fund (*www.accessfund.org*).

Because of the uncertain nature of the climbing access at Queen Creek, I've chosen a selection of climbs at the Mine area and the Road area for inclusion in this guide. The Mine has by far the largest concentration of quality, moderate lines at Queen Creek. In hopes that access to

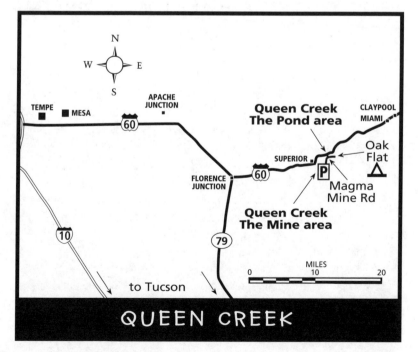

this wonderful area is preserved, I've included a number of climbs here. In case access to this premier area becomes restricted in the future, I've also covered some of the best moderate climbs the Road area has to offer, at the Pond. The climbing here is excellent, but given that the routes lie directly above a busy highway, the ambiance falls short of that at the Mine. Interestingly enough, the Pond and most of the other major crags in the Road area are owned by Resolution Copper. Continued access to these areas is by no means assured, but at least the areas don't lie directly above the proposed mine. Many additional quality 5.6–5.10a lines exist at the Mine area, and Marty Karabin's guidebook *The Rock Jock's Guide to Queen Creek Canyon* covers them. The Magma Gardens area has a particularly good selection of moderate routes.

Queen Creek is an excellent example of the constant threats to access that exist even for premier climbing areas located on public land. If we stay informed and involved, many access issues can be resolved in a beneficial way. The Access Fund is a national organization that tries to coordinate such efforts. Here is hoping that we will all be able to enjoy the wonderful climbing at the Mine area for many years to come.

QUEEN CREEK BETA

Drive time from Tucson ▲ 2 hours
Drive time from Phoenix ▲ 1 hour
Drive time from Flagstaff ▲ 3 hours

Getting there: From Phoenix, follow US 60 to Superior. From Tucson, approach Superior by taking SR 79 to US 60 at Florence Junction and on to Superior from there. From Superior, follow US 60 east, through a tunnel, to reach the climbs. To reach the Mine area, drive 4 miles east of Superior to the Magma Mine Road (milepost 231). Turn right (south). Continue south and west on the Magma Mine Road for 1.8 miles to a dirt pullout on the left side of the road, 500 feet before the gate to the mine. For climbs at the Pond, drive 2.5 miles east of Superior on US 60 and park at the third pullout on the right (south) side of the road after the tunnel. This is at milepost 229.3, and it is distinguished by the large island of rock in the middle of the huge pullout.

Approach: The approach to each area is described in its respective section of the guide. All routes at both the Mine and the Pond may be easily reached in 5–15 minutes of walking.

Season and Elevation: Queen Creek Canyon is at 3800–4000 feet.

The comfortable climbing season runs from September through April. Winter climbing here is generally comfortable, but be prepared for the occasional chilly day. It's best to pick a different spot for those hot summer months! Climbs at the Mine face a variety of directions, and I've listed the direction each climb faces to help you find shade or sun according to your needs. Most of the routes at the Pond face south or west, with the few exceptions noted in the climb description.

Regulations: All climbs at the Mine currently lie on land belonging to the Tonto National Forest. See the introduction for an access alert regarding climbs here. The Pond is on land owned by Resolution Copper Company. It has permitted climbing access in the past, but given its current plans to develop a huge mine in the area, this situation could change. Contact the Access Fund or Friends of Queen Creek for the current access situation.

Camping: Nice, free camping can be found at Oak Flat Campground less than 2 miles from the climbs at both areas. Turn south onto Magma Mine Road at milepost 231. The campground is on your left, 0.1 mile down Magma Mine Road. Oak Flat has portable toilet facilities but no water or trash services. Please pack out all of your trash, as the maintenance of this free camping facility depends on all of us.

Gear: Most climbs are sport routes, requiring only quickdraws, but bring your rack to enjoy some of the cracks. All of the climbs listed are a half-rope length or less. The nearest gear stores are in Phoenix, 60 miles away.

Emergency Services: The nearest telephone is located in Superior. The nearest emergency medical facility is CVCH Superior Clinic at 14 N. Magma Ave. in Superior (520-689-2423). The larger Cobre Valley Community Hospital is at 5880 S. Hospital Road, Globe, 16 miles to the east (928-425-3261).

Kids and Dogs: The Mine is a particularly nice area to bring the family and the pooch since the camping is nearby for those who don't want to be at the crag all day. The approaches are easy, and all climbs are single pitch. The steep, loose approach to climbs at the Pond is less friendly.

The Mine Area

The climbing here takes place on a maze of small spires and buttresses scattered about in a beautiful desert environment. The approach hikes are short and pleasant.

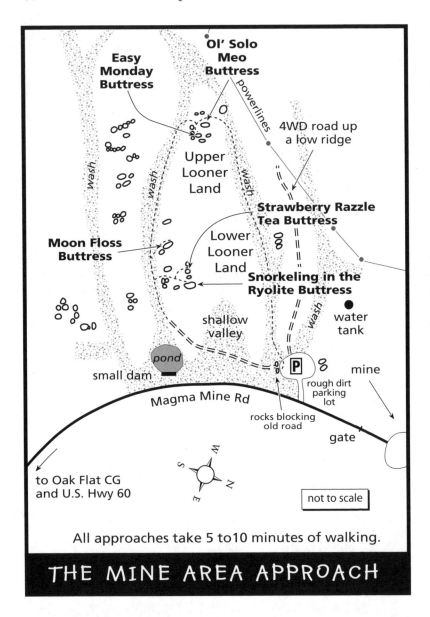

Ol' Solo Meo Buttress

Easy Monday Buttress

powerlines

4WD road up a low ridge

Upper Looner Land

wash

wash

wash

Strawberry Razzle Tea Buttress

Lower Looner Land

Moon Floss Buttress

Snorkeling in the Ryolite Buttress

shallow valley

wash

water tank

pond

small dam

mine

Magma Mine Rd

P

rough dirt parking lot

rocks blocking old road

gate

to Oak Flat CG and U.S. Hwy 60

not to scale

All approaches take 5 to10 minutes of walking.

THE MINE AREA APPROACH

LOWER LOONER LAND

Lower Looner Land has one of the best groupings of moderate climbs at Queen Creek. To reach it, head out the left side of the parking lot

top of Strawberry Razzle Tea Buttress

LOWER LOONER LAND

(southeast) onto a dirt road blocked by several big boulders. After passing through a shallow valley, the road curves right into a wash. Lower Looner Land is the first grouping of large pinnacles on your right as you head up the wash.

Snorkeling in the Rhyolite Buttress
This is the largest buttress in Lower Looner Land, with three distinctive blocks on top. The climb faces west.

1. SNORKELING IN THE RHYOLITE 5.5 ★★ Sport
FA: Bob Pettit, Steve Joyner 1990
This very enjoyable route follows the line of 3 bolts on the left side of the buttress to a double-bolt anchor. The first bolt is high off the ground, but the moves below it are moderate. Rappel from top. 3 bolts, 40 feet.

Strawberry Razzle Tea Buttress
This is two buttresses west and at the same elevation as *Snorkeling in the Rhyolite*. A faint trail through the manzanitas leads up a narrow gully to the buttress. Climbs face west.

Terri Cook is Snorkeling in the Rhyolite.

2. BOXCAR BOB 5.6 ★

FA: Eric Agaciewski, Steve Agaciewski, Bob Blair 1994

Climb past 1 bolt on the left side of the face, then up past a series of horizontal cracks that take stoppers and small to medium cams to the *Strawberry Razzle Tea* anchor. Rappel. 40 feet.

3. STRAWBERRY RAZZLE TEA 5.8 ★★ Sport

FA: Eric Agaciewski, Steve Agaciewski, Bob Blair 1994

Follow the line of 4 bolts up the steep right side of the buttress. The small but very positive holds make this route fun. Double-bolt rap. 4 bolts, 40 feet.

SNORKELING IN THE RHYOLITE

STRAWBERRY RAZZLE TEA BUTTRESS

Moon Floss Buttress

This is the westernmost large buttress in the Lower Looner Land group, low on the slope. The west face of the buttress is broken into two sections by a prominent chimney. There are four lines of bolts on the larger left section. The three leftmost are described below, from left to right. *Moon Floss* is the lone bolt line on the narrower right section of cliff. It is possible to top-rope *Mary Jane* and *Grasping for Straws* by walking and scrambling around the back (east) side of the rock to top anchors.

4. MARY JANE 5.9 ★ Sport
FA: Dana Hollister 1994
Climb the line of 3 bolts on the left side of the face. A sling and

Grappling with the off-width crack of Grand Titon. *(Photo: Terri Cook)*

medium to large cams are necessary for the belay. **Descent:** Walk off the back. 3 bolts, 40 feet.

5. GRASPING FOR STRAWS 5.9+ ★★ Sport
FA: Bob Pettit, Steve Joyner 1990
Climb the line of 4 bolts to the right of *Mary Jane*. The climbing is steep and delicate. **Descent:** Rap off the double-bolt anchor, or walk off the east side. 4 bolts, 45 feet.

6. THE NEW COMER 5.10a ★★ Sport
Climb thought-provoking moves past 4 bolts to the right of *Grasping for Straws*, past a loose, left-facing flake. **Descent:** Rap or walk off. 4 bolts, 45 feet.

7. GRAND TITON 5.7 ★
FA: Greg Opland, Gary Youngblood 1992
This is a fun and unusual climb for Queen Creek. Climb the prominent chimney to the off-width crack that splits the buttress. Stoppers and several large cams are needed to lead it. This climb may also be top-roped off the *Moon Floss* anchors if you bring a #2 or #2½ cam for a directional at the top of the crack. **Descent:** Rap off the *Moon Floss* anchors or walk off. 50 feet.

8. MOON FLOSS 5.8 ★★ Sport
FA: Bob Pettit, Steve Joyner 1990

Beautiful climbing leads past 3 bolts up the narrow buttress right of *Grand Titon*. The climbing eases considerably above the second bolt. **Descent:** Rap or walk off. 3 bolts, 50 feet.

UPPER LOONER LAND

To reach Upper Looner Land from the car, go straight ahead through the far end of the parking lot (southwest) up the wash to the left of the 4WD road that climbs up the low ridge. A few hundred yards up the wash you encounter a 40-foot-tall buttress (the Entrance Boulder) guarding the wash's left side. Turn left (south) just before this buttress and cross a low saddle. The climbing is on the buttresses that cluster around the saddle.

To approach Upper Looner Land from Lower Looner Land, continue up the wash a few hundred yards to the next cluster of large rocks on the right side of the wash. These rocks, which lie around a low saddle, are Upper Looner Land.

Easy Monday Buttress

This 45-foot-tall buttress is distinguished by the vertical crack that runs right up the center. It lies 100 feet beyond Ol' Solo Meo Buttress, immediately north of the tallest rock in Upper Looner Land (the Spinal Tap Buttress). The climbs face west and are shielded from the sun a bit longer than most.

9. EASY MONDAY 5.7 R ★

FA: Marty Karabin 1996

This is the face climb on the left side of the buttress. It's a long way to the first bolt. The crux comes between the 2 bolts. Above the second bolt you reach a crack that takes stoppers, and a bigger crack above that will accept large cams. **Descent:** Rap from the double-bolt anchor.

10. COULDN'T STAND THE WEATHER 5.8 ★

FA: Jeff Giek, Gordon Ogden 1989

Moderate face climbing past 1 bolt leads to the central crack on the buttress. Stoppers and small to medium cams offer good protection past

Couldn't Stand the Weather *begins with face moves and ends with a steep crack. (Photo: Terri Cook)*

several interesting moves up the crack. **Descent:** Rap from the double-bolt anchor.

Ol' Solo Meo Buttress

This is the 40-foot-tall, pyramid-shaped buttress, cut by two nearly horizontal cracks, which lies at the saddle. Three lines of bolts are found on the west face.

The headframe of the old mine stands above the beautiful countryside of The Mine area. The new mine slated to take its place will cause this area to collapse into a giant underground pit.

11. THE BYRD 5.3 TR

Follow the low-angle ramp left of *Ol' Solo Meo*, traversing right to finish on *Ol' Solo Meo*. This climb is top-roped from the *Ol' Solo Meo* anchor.

12. OL' SOLO MEO 5.6 ★★ Sport

FA: Doug Smith 1990

This is the very enjoyable pocketed face along the leftmost bolt line. Rap off the double-bolt anchor.

13. UNKNOWN CLIMB 5.7+ ★ Sport

Delicate moves lead past the first 2 bolts to easier climbing above. This is the middle line of 4 bolts. Rap from the double-bolt anchor.

14. RIDERS ON THE STORM 5.9+ ★ Sport

FA: Marc Nielsen, Tyler Treece 1991

Footholds are in short supply at the start of this thin face climb up the right-hand bolt line. Climb past 2 bolts, then veer left to a third bolt. Rap off the double-bolt anchor. This climb shares top anchors with *Unknown Climb*, so it can be easily top-roped.

The Pond Area

The Pond offers the highest concentration of moderate routes at the Road area. The climbing is excellent and the scenery is beautiful, but the ambiance of the place is compromised by the roar of traffic on US 60 below the climbs. The approach is short but mildly unpleasant. It begins by walking east along the south side of the highway a few hundred yards to a small bridge. Here you need to get to the north side of the highway, and you have two equally unpleasant choices: Either scramble down the steep, crumbling embankment to the wash and walk under the bridge or run across the highway.

Once on the north side of the highway you are presented with two more choices. All but the last two climbs listed here lie up and left of this wash. The shortest and most direct approach is to follow the steep trail up the slope on the left, below a wall covered with hard, bolted climbs (Lower Pond Wall). As you reach the base of this wall, descend west through a notch in the broken rock below the climbs and then continue to follow the trail as it angles up the slope to the northwest. The trail then leads up a scruffy gully, depositing you on a large platform at the base of *Pocket Puzzle*. This approach takes about 10 minutes. Alternatively, once you cross the road

you can walk up the flat trail directly ahead for 30 seconds to a small, dirty pond. Scramble up the slabs right (east) of this pond to an upper pond. *Natural Wonder* and *Beer and Dead Animals* lie just to the right of this upper pond. To reach the other climbs follow the trail to the left (west), past numerous bolted routes, stepping around an exposed corner at one point. The first climb you reach after stepping around this corner is *The Cowboy*, and a short distance beyond lies the platform below *Pocket Puzzle*.

Most of the routes here face southwest, making this a great cold weather area.

THE NOTHINGS AREA

1. NEXT TO NOTHING 5.4 ★★ Sport
To reach this climb hike left (northwest) from the platform below *Pocket Puzzle* past several buttresses until you reach a buttress with a distinctive right-angling crack splitting its lower right side. This fun climb ascends the shorter, low-angled face to the right of this crack, past 4 bolts to a double-bolt anchor. 4 bolts, 40 feet.

2. NOTHING'S LEFT 5.8 ★★ Sport
This is the left line of bolts up a clean, narrow face 70 feet right of

Next to Nothing. The crux is surmounting the bulge to get on the wall. Pass 5 bolts en route to a double-bolt top anchor. 5 bolts, 45 feet.

3. NOTHING'S RIGHT 5.7 ★★ Sport

This is a nearly identical but slightly easier twin to *Nothing's Left*. It tackles the right line of bolts on the same wall. Rap from the double-bolt anchor. 5 bolts, 45 feet.

SAPPY LOVE SONG AREA

4. FAT BOY GOES TO THE POND 5.6 ★ Sport

This route ascends the short, narrow buttress with a prominent horizontal ledge 10 feet up that lies about 100 feet down and right from *Nothing's Right*. The first bolt lies above the horizontal, making the beginning slightly runout. Rap from a double-bolt anchor with chains. 2 bolts, 35 feet.

5. SAPPY LOVE SONG 5.8 ★★ Sport
FA: Marty Karabin

This is one of the best routes at the Pond, but beware of the fairly long runouts between bolts. The route follows the left of two bolt lines on the larger face 30 feet right of *Fat Boy Goes to the Pond*. The crux is getting past the overhang after clipping the first bolt, but the climbing remains interesting throughout. 4 bolts to a double-bolt anchor. 55 feet.

6. FOLLOW YOUR HEART 5.7 ★★ Sport

This climb takes the right-hand bolt line on the *Sappy Love Song* face. Begin on top of a pointy fallen boulder beneath the wall 6 feet right of *Sappy Love Song*. 6 bolts to a double-bolt anchor. 50 feet.

McNeill Mann enjoys Sappy Love Song's *steep, pocketed face. (Photo: Chance Traub)*

7. CHRISTMAS CHOCOLATE 5.6 ★ Sport

This climb ascends the line of 5 bolts on the narrow, low-angled face between two cracks 8 feet right of *Follow Your Heart*. The climbing is moderate up to a difficult crux past the last bolt where the holds become considerably smaller. Rappel from the double-bolt anchor. 6 bolts, 65 feet.

POCKET PUZZLE AREA

8. POCKET PUZZLE 5.10a ★★★ Sport

This is one of the best routes at Queen Creek. It provides amazing pocket climbing up a steep to bulging, west-facing wall. The route lies about 200 feet down and right from *Christmas Chocolate*, and the large, flat platform at its base is a distinctive feature. Climb the pocketed face up the leftmost line of 8 bolts (the ones that aren't orange) to a double-bolt anchor. 8 bolts, 70 feet.

9. POCKET PULLING PANSIES ON PARADE 5.10a ★★ Sport

This is a fun but somewhat squeezed line that ascends the line of 8 orange bolts up the face 3 feet right of *Pocket Puzzle* and immediately left of a scooped overhanging wall. The crux is low down on the steep wall, with lower-angle rock above. It finishes at a double-bolt anchor. 8 bolts, 70 feet.

10. POCKET WARMER 5.6 ★ Sport

This route ascends a narrow pillar 70 feet right of *Pocket Puzzle*, around the corner. It faces west and lies immediately right of a large wall with 4 bolt lines. The bolts on this route have black hangers. Rappel from a double-bolt anchor. 5 bolts, 45 feet.

POCKET PUZZLE AREA

11. THE COWBOY 5.10a ★ Sport

This short, pumpy route faces southeast. It lies 100 feet right of *Pocket Warmer*, around the next corner. It ascends an easy, left-angling ramp up to a steep face with 3 bolts. Climb quickly past the bolts, before your energy wanes, to the cold-shut top anchor. 3 bolts, 45 feet.

Opposite: Chance Traub enjoys the Queen Creek megaclassic Pocket Puzzle.

THE COWBOY

⑪

NATURAL WONDER AREA
----

12. NATURAL WONDER 5.8 ★

This route and *Beer and Dead Animals* lie on the prominent buttress right of the Upper Pond. See the introductory material for the Pond for approach directions to the Upper Pond. From there, walk up and right to the base of the obvious, curving crack. Ascend the crack as it widens from fingers and hands to off-width. Rappel using the bolts on top of

Beer and Dead Animals. The crack protects with medium to large cams, up to a #5 Camalot. 45 feet.

13. BEER AND DEAD ANIMALS 5.9 ★ Sport

This is a short, strenuous climb up pockets to a finish on slopers. It is the rightmost of three bolt lines on the face right of *Natural Wonder.* It ends at a cold-shut anchor. 2 bolts, 25 feet.

NATURAL WONDER AREA

Pinnacle Peak

Metropolitan Phoenix is sprinkled with numerous small climbing areas. Pinnacle Peak offers more classic routes than any of them. Short granite crack and face routes are the name of the game here. The rock is 1.4-billion-year-old Ruin Granite, which is very coarse and offers excellent friction. Pinnacle Peak forms the centerpiece for a Scottsdale park. Pinnacle Peak's proximity to metropolitan Phoenix, its quick and easy approach, and the abundance of quality routes make it an ideal location for a quick after-work climbing session for Phoenix residents or a place to tick a lot of routes for visitors passing through the area.

After being closed for seven years, Pinnacle Peak was reopened to the public in April 2002. A large chunk of land, including Pinnacle Peak, had been sold to a developer in 1995 with the provision that the developer donate a portion of land, including the peak, to the city of Scottsdale to become a public park.

When the developer got cold feet on the original agreement, members of the climbing community were among those who, through their persistence and diplomacy, got the park opened. Climbers have built and stabilized climbing access trails from the popular main hiking trail that runs 1.75 miles one-way through this 150-acre park. This main trail has well-designed and informative signs describing the flora, fauna, geology, and cultural history of the area. The

On top of the AMC Boulder

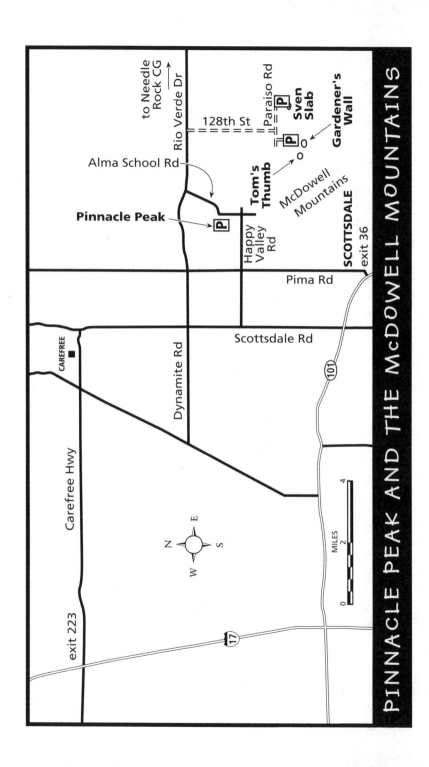

PINNACLE PEAK AND THE McDOWELL MOUNTAINS

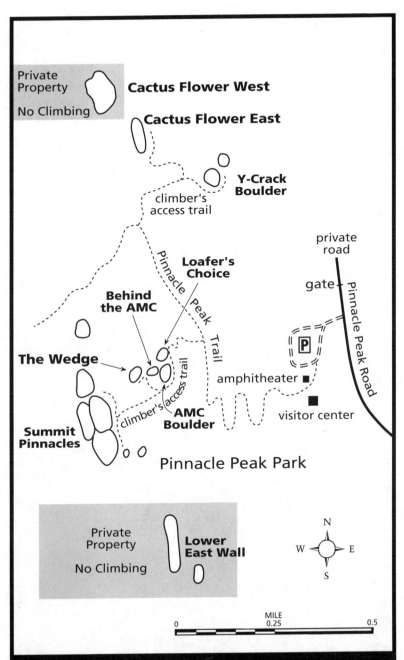

Private
Property

No Climbing

Cactus Flower West

Cactus Flower East

**Y-Crack
Boulder**

climber's
access trail

Pinnacle Peak Trail

private
road

gate

Pinnacle Peak Road

**Loafer's
Choice**

**Behind
the AMC**

P

The Wedge

amphitheater

climber's access trail

**AMC
Boulder**

visitor center

**Summit
Pinnacles**

Pinnacle Peak Park

Private
Property

No Climbing

**Lower
East Wall**

N
W   E
S

MILE
0.25

0   0.5

PINNACLE PEAK APPROACH

park stands as an unusual and inspiring example of a city's willingness to support and peacefully coexist with the climbing community. Please be a good steward of our sport and respect the city's regulations as well as the rights of the surrounding landowners who may never have imagined themselves living in a place where climbers play in their backyards.

The manicured trails and the urban setting make Pinnacle Peak feel pretty tame, but beware that this is an unpredictable and potentially dangerous environment. Rattlesnakes and scorpions abound, and the Summit Pinnacle has more than its share of bees. If you are allergic, come prepared, and even if you're not, be mindful of the stinging company!

PINNACLE PEAK BETA

Drive time from Tucson ▲ 2 hours
Drive time from Phoenix ▲ 0–30 minutes
Drive time from Flagstaff ▲ 2 hours

Getting there: From I-10 or I-17, take the Loop 101 freeway north or east, respectively, to exit 36 (Pima Road and Princess Drive). Go 4.5 miles north on Pima Road to Happy Valley Road. Turn right (east) and drive 1.9 miles to a stop sign and turn left on Alma School Road. Go 1 mile north, then turn left on Pinnacle Peak Road. Drive 0.4 mile to the Pinnacle Peak parking lot on the left.

Approach: 10–15 minutes. From the parking lot, hike up the immaculately groomed and very crowded trail for approximately 0.3 mile to a posted climber's trail on the left to reach the Loafer's Choice, the AMC Boulder, the Wedge, and the Summit Pinnacles. Continue an additional 0.2 mile on the main trail to another marked climber's trail on the right to reach the Y-Crack Boulder and Cactus Flower East.

Season and Elevation: The trailhead is at 2570 feet and the summit tops out at 3170 feet. Because of its low elevation, Pinnacle Peak is a great winter and spring venue. Summers are so hot that climbing is uncomfortable, but because routes face in all directions, you can still find some early or late shade if you are desperate.

Regulations: Pinnacle Peak is within a Scottsdale park, which is open dawn to dusk. Please stay on established access trails. The Lower East Wall and Cactus Flower West are on private property and are not open to climbing. Please respect the landowners. There is plenty of good climbing within the bounds of the city park.

Camping: The nearest campground is Needle Rock in the Tonto

National Forest and, a short distance farther, in the McDowell Mountain Regional Park. See the McDowell Mountains chapter for directions to these areas. This is an urban area; in addition to camping, everything from inexpensive hotels to fancy resorts abounds within easy driving distance.

Food and Supplies: Ah, the joys of the urban climbing experience—plenty of grocery stores and restaurants to choose from!

Gear: A standard rack and single rope will suffice. There are a lot of wide cracks here, so bring some large cams.

Emergency Services: The closest hospital is the Mayo Clinic Hospital in Scottsdale at 5777 E. Mayo Boulevard, a short distance south of the Loop 101 highway at 56th Street. (480-515-6296)

Kids and Dogs: This is a great place for kids and nonclimbers who may want to enjoy a stroll on the hiking trail. Dogs are not allowed in the park.

The Wedge

This is the impressive wedge of rock that lies near the top of the ridge that descends east from the summit of the peak. Eyebolts on top facilitate a short rappel to the ground.

THE WEDGE

1. HILITER 5.7 R ★ Sport
FA: Lance Daugherty, Dane Daugherty 1967

This route lies on the northeast face, around the left corner from where the trail reaches the rock. Climb past 2 bolts to easier but runout climbing and the top. 2 bolts, 40 feet.

2. REDEMPTION 5.9 ★★
Sport
FA: Lance Daugherty, Dane Daugherty 1968

This enjoyable face climb moves up and left past 3 bolts, then back right via hand-over-hand on the ridge to large rap bolts on the small summit. If you prefer, it is easy to top-rope this and *Naked Edge* after leading *Hiliter*. 3 bolts, 40 feet.

3. NAKED EDGE 5.9 ★★★
FA: Larry Treiber 1974

Start in a lieback finger crack on the right side of the clean face, then face climb past 3 bolts to the

Climbers cling to the tiny perch atop The Wedge.

The Summit Pinnacles loom behind Laura Plaut as she ascends Redemption *on The Wedge.*

top. Good stopper placements are available in the bottom crack. 3 bolts, 40 feet.

BEHIND THE AMC

This is the small rock that lies behind and above the AMC Boulder, which is distinctive. A very large, single eyebolt provides the top anchor for a short rappel.

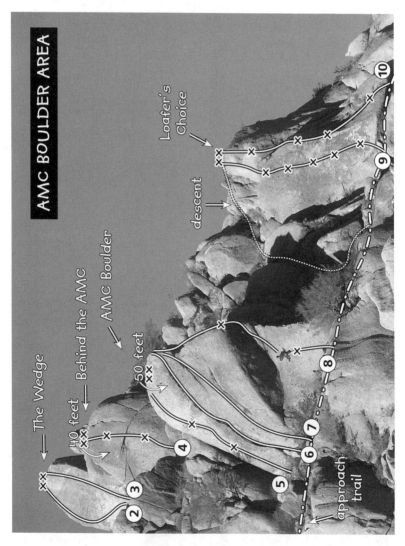

4. DELAYED FLIGHT 5.8 ★★ Sport

FA: Chuck Hill, Scherry Duncan 1984

Two bolts separated by a horizontal crack, which takes gear if you want to take the time to place it, protect this short but enjoyable face route. 2 bolts, 40 feet.

AMC Boulder

This is the most distinctive of the smaller rocks clustered along the east ridge below the main cliff. It is distinguished by an aesthetic, right-curving crack (*Varicose*). The approach trail to the main cliff passes immediately below the rock. Eyebolts on the summit provide an anchor for the single-rope rappel.

5. REUNION 5.8 R or 5.8 TR ★

FA: Ted Olsen 1985

Climb past 2 bolts on the narrow face to the left of *Varicose*. The first bolt is pretty far off the deck, but this route is easily top-roped after climbing *Varicose*. 2 bolts, 50 feet.

Laura Plaut delicately edges up the steep friction slab of Delayed Flight.

6. VARICOSE 5.6 ★★

FA: Arizona Mountaineering Club members
Follow the obvious right-leaning crack. Bring a standard rack to a
#4 cam. 50 feet.

7. RUPTURE 5.10b TR ★

FA: John Ficker, Ken Akers, Glen Dickinson 1981
This route ascends the face right of *Varicose* and is easily top-roped
from the bolt anchor on top of the AMC Boulder. 50 feet.

8. MICKEY MANTLE 5.8 ★★

FA: Arizona Mountaineering Club members
Pass 1 bolt on the face 30 feet right of *Varicose* to a horn. Stoppers,
RPs, or small cams serve as intermediate protection here, along with a
long sling to lasso the horn. From the horn, move up onto the steep face
above, clipping a second bolt along the way. 2 bolts, 50 feet.

LOAFER'S CHOICE SLAB

This is the first rock you pass on the climber's approach trail that is large
enough to host routes. It is on your right as you scramble over boulders
in the first narrow portion of the approach trail. If you reach the AMC
Boulder, you have passed it by. Backtrack 10 yards from the *Mickey Mantle*
face, and you will be staring directly at the brown slab of Loafer's Choice.
The descent takes you down the gully to the left (southwest) of the rock.

9. LOAFER'S CHOICE 5.10a ★★★ Sport

FA: John Ficker, Jim Zahn, Jim Waugh, Glen Dickinson 1979
This climb tackles the rock's clean south face. Climb past 5 bolts, or
top-rope the route by scrambling up the gully to the left of the climb.
5 bolts, 50 feet.

10. DEAD MEAT 5.7 ★★

FA: John Ficker, Steve Smelser 1982
Ascend the arête immediately right of *Loafer's Choice*. Move up a slab
on the right side of the arête to the first bolt, then move up and place a
#4 Camalot in a horizontal before stepping over the roof. Follow more
bolts on the face and arête above, step onto the summit block, and clip
a final bolt before the top. 4 bolts, 50 feet.

Ascending the arête on Dead Meat

Summit Pinnacles

This is the tallest and most prominent rock, forming the summit of Pinnacle Peak. There are actually several separate spires, with a broad shoulder extending to the south that is known as the Sundeck Boulder. These climbs all face south or east, offering sun for the cooler winter months or afternoon shade when things heat up. Approach via the marked climber's approach trail. There are so many monstrously large eyebolts on the summits that you can pretty much choose your favorite descent route. The best descents are listed for each climb.

1. BIRTHDAY PARTY 5.7 ★★
FA: Dana Hollister, Chuck Parker, Pete Noebels 1974
This route is located on the Sundeck Boulder, the low shoulder of rock

left of the main summit pinnacle. It begins in a dihedral below the left edge of the prominent roof. Climb up the face past 1 bolt, then follow a right-leaning crack to an awkward stance below the roof. Pull the roof via a vertical hand crack, where #½, #3, and #4 Camalots are useful. A descent can be made by scrambling left and down around the left side of the Sundeck Boulder or by scrambling right to the rappel anchors at the top of *South Crack*'s first pitch. One rope will get you down that rappel. Beware of bees. 70 feet.

2. SOUTH CRACK 5.3 ★★★

FA: Ed George, Bill McMorris 1947

Can 5.3 get any better?! This classic route begins in a less-than-classic chimney that marks the right side of the Sundeck Boulder. **Pitch One:** Go up the obvious fourth-class chimney to a double-bolt belay on a ledge just below the top of the Sundeck Boulder. 50 feet. **Pitch Two:** Step left and up, around a block, then continue up a wide crack that ascends the summit pinnacle. A mix of diverse crack and face climbing leads up the crack and over an airy chasm that cleaves the summit pinnacle in half. Move left here, onto the face leading to the left summit. 150 feet. Stoppers and cams to a #2 Camalot are needed. **Descent:** There are a variety of rap bolts available for the descent, all of which require only 1 rope. The standard rap leads north off the summit to a prominent notch, where a short scramble leads to a second set of anchors that land you on the ground far north of your starting point. *Note:* If there aren't any parties behind you, a more efficient descent down the route via three single-rope rappels is possible.

3. SILHOUETTE 5.8 ★★★

Ascend the first pitch of *South Crack* and the initial wide crack section of that route's second pitch. When you reach a stance below the beautiful slab on the left, step left and face climb past 4 bolts to the top. Descend as for *South Crack*.

Golf courses and high-end homes separate Pinnacle Peak from the crags of the McDowell Mountains, seen here in the distance.

4. CHUG-A-LUG 5.8 ★★
FA: Chuck Parker 1973

The classic first pitch will provide a quick fix for crack climbers dreaming of Canyonlands. This route lies in the alcove right (north) of the main summit pinnacle. You can't miss the splitter hand crack that lies on a fin of rock just left of the approach gully. **Pitch One:** Ascend the short, steep, strenuous hand crack to a belay stance at a horizontal crack. 30 feet. **Pitch Two:** Step up into a thin dihedral crack immediately right of the wide chimney. 30 feet. The initial face moves into the crack on this pitch are not well protected, and the climbing isn't really that good, anyway. It's easy to skip this second pitch by scrambling down and right from the top of the first pitch. If you do want to climb it, it is no problem to combine the two pitches.

5. CHUTES AND LADDERS 5.7 ★★
FA: Chuck Parker, Doug Rickard 1973

This thoroughly enjoyable, left-trending crack eats up nuts at the bottom and then moves right up lower-angle, enjoyable climbing to belay bolts at the top. 100 feet. It is reached by moving up the approach gully north of the summit pinnacle to the base of the pretty finger crack that angles up the face to the right of the gully. To descend, walk down and east 15 feet to another set of bolts that anchor the single-rope rappel southeast to the base of the climb.

Y-Crack Boulder

This distinctive boulder sits on the crest of a small hill to the east of the main hiker's trail north of the main summit rock. A marked climber's access trail leaves the hiking trail directly across from the Y-Crack rock. This rock looks small and benign from a distance, but the Y-Crack face is impressive and overhanging when you stand beneath it. Summit bolts provide rappel anchors.

1. Y-CRACK 5.9 ★★ TR
FA: Pete Noebels, Dennis Abbink, Larry Treiber 1977

This is a challenging off-width lead that requires several tube chocks to adequately protect. Consider top-roping it instead by climbing any of

Y-CRACK BOULDER FRONT SIDE

the other routes on the rock. On top rope, it provides good off-width practice, or you can lieback a hidden flake to avoid the thrutching! 50 feet.

2. TURTLE PISS 5.6 ★
FA: Steve Haire, Steve Shultz 1984

This route and *Corona Club* and *Jam on Jam* lie on the back side of the Y-Crack rock. Two bolts lead up a clean, fairly low-angle face here to a double-bolt rappel anchor. 30 feet.

3. CORONA CLUB 5.9 ★

This route takes 2 bolts up the steeper face to the right of *Turtle Piss*. It is very easy to top-rope the climb after climbing *Turtle Piss*. 30 feet.

4. JAM ON JAM 5.5
FA: Steve White, Tink Golamb, Bill Heer 1983

This is the leaning hand crack immediately right of *Corona Club*. It is stiff for a 5.5. 35 feet.

Y-CRACK BOULDER
BACK SIDE

Cactus Flower East

What the Cactus Flower East area lacks in height of climbs, it easily makes up for in terms of sheer quantity of moderate climbs, one right next to the other. None of these routes is classic, but they are all fun. You can lead them or, if you're willing to hike to the top to set up gear anchors, top-rope them. Descend from the top of the upper-tier climbs by walking off to the climber's right and from the lower-tier climbs by walking off to the climber's left or right.

UPPER TIER

1. ANARCHIST'S DELIGHT 5.8
This is the 30-foot crack located 30 feet left of *Zenolith*, on the taller portion of the upper tier. 30 feet.

2. ZENOLITH 5.9 ★
FA: Jim Waugh, John Ficker 1986
This fun climb tackles the knobby face past zenoliths and left-angling seams past 2 bolts. 20 feet.

3. BANANA SPLIT 5.6
This climb ascends the vertical crack 15 feet right of *Zenolith*. Climb past a small roof and up the crack. The route uses small- to medium-sized protection. 20 feet.

4. MIXED FEELINGS 5.7
FA: Gary Youngblood, Noel Aronov, Jan Holdeman 1986
This route ascends the discontinuous seams directly above the lower-tier climb, *Banana Crack*, and 5 feet right of *Banana Split*. Pass a horizontal crack en route. The climb takes small to medium protection, and you should save a medium-sized cam for the top belay. 20 feet.

LOWER TIER

5. WORM 5.6
This is the leftmost hand crack on the lower tier. It takes small- to medium-sized protection in its 20 feet.

6. FASCIST PIG 5.9
This route takes the thin crack 10 feet right of *Worm*. Climb the crack past 1 bolt to the top. Bring small- to medium-sized gear. 20 feet.

7. KING OF PAIN 5.10a ★
FA: Chuck Hill, Pat Reineke 1986
For a short wall, this climb is pretty impressive. Ascend the slightly

CACTUS FLOWER EAST

overhanging wall past 2 bolts to the top. The bolts are spaced pretty far apart, so most folks will prefer to top-rope this one. 35 feet.

8. TWO CAMS AND JAM 5.10a TR
FA: Chuck Hill, Pat Reineke 1986
This crack climb shares a start with *Banana Crack*, continuing straight up where *Banana Crack* arches right. Most folks will want to top-rope this climb, but if you want to lead it, bring some big gear to protect the wide-crack start. 35 feet.

9. BANANA CRACK 5.9 ★
This is probably the most enjoyable climb at Cactus Flower East. It ascends the obvious, right-arching crack in the center of the lower tier then climbs the short face above. You will need medium and large cams to protect this on lead. Alternatively, you can easily top-rope it using #3 and #4 Camalots for the top anchor. 35 feet.

10. LIVE OAK 5.7
This route takes the right-angling hand crack located about 70 feet right of *Banana Crack*, just right of a large block. It takes small to medium protection. 30 feet.

11. PALO VERDE 5.7
This is the next hand crack on the wall, 20 feet right of *Live Oak*. It angles left over a bulge and passes the left side of a prominent horizontal crack. The route protects with medium-sized gear. 30 feet.

12. POMEY DIRECT 5.9 TR
This is the face 5 feet right of *Palo Verde*, which is best top-roped. 30 feet.

13. CAT CLAW 5.6
Begin this route below an off-width crack that begins partway up the wall. Ascend the face to reach the crack, then the off-width. Bring some large gear. 30 feet.

McDowell Mountains

The McDowell Mountains compose an urban outback. Although the upscale golf courses and subdivisions of Scottsdale, Phoenix's most fashionable suburb, are creeping uncomfortably close, the crags are accessed via a rutted dirt road, and the area still feels as if it were in the middle of nowhere. The McDowells contain the largest concentration of climbs and longest routes in the immediate Phoenix area. The rock here is known to geologists as the Ruin Granite, a 1.4-billion-year-old hunk of granite that is extremely coarse-grained, providing exceptional friction. You can friction climb your way up some unbelievably steep faces here! And, like most granite, this rock fractures along some very beautiful cracks. The result is one of the finest climbing areas in the Phoenix area.

The McDowell Mountains are littered with dozens of climbable rocks. It would require many excursions to explore all the climbing this compact mountain range has to offer, but most of the climbing activity here centers on the three best crags: Sven Slab, Gardener's Wall, and Tom's Thumb. Sven Slab offers the most accessible climbing, consisting mostly of slabby face routes 40–100 feet long that are accessible with an easy 5- to 10-minute approach hike. Gardener's Wall is a clean, massive slab of rock that hosts crack and face routes up to 300 feet long, the longest climbs around Phoenix. You will work up a sweat approaching it, but

Matt Moss tiptoeing up Cakewalk *at Sven Slab*

Although the developments of Phoenix and Scottsdale lap at the feet of the McDowell Mountains, the urban rat race feels miles away as you tread the summit ridges.

a good trail makes the 35-minute approach hike relatively painless. Tom's Thumb, an ostentatious protrusion of granite perched high on the ridge crest, is the most striking climbing objective. It is generally considered the best climbing cliff in the Phoenix area, making it worth the hot, steep 50-minute approach.

Most McDowell face climbs were bolted during the 1970s, and like most slab climbs of that vintage the bolts are usually spaced about 20 feet apart, causing some modern climbers to find the runouts long. Of more concern is that on Gardener's Wall and Tom's Thumb, with the exception of a few anchor bolts, nobody has bothered to replace the original bolts from the initial ascents in the 1960s and 1970s. These rusting relics will probably hold a fall, but it would be prudent if someone replaced them with some modern, stainless-steel hardware.

Access to the climbing has been a significant issue here, as it has throughout the Phoenix area since the suburban sprawl began engulfing one formerly remote mountain range after another. Fortunately, the residents of Scottsdale had the vision to pass bond initiatives in 1990, 1995, and 1998 that created and then expanded the McDowell Sonoran Preserve. All the major climbing cliffs lie within the boundaries of the original preserve, but throughout the 1990s access problems continued because of disputes with the owners of the land hosting the trailheads. Fortunately, the main trailheads were included in the expanded preserve planning boundary that was established in 1998, and access is no longer

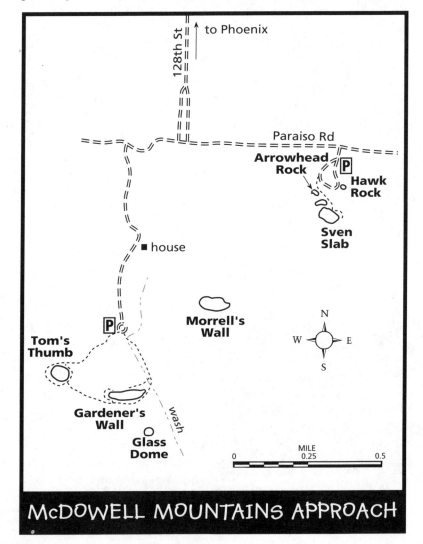

McDOWELL MOUNTAINS APPROACH

Gardener's Wall

approach
trail

Tom's Thumb

← to Sven Slab

parking

MCDOWELL MOUNTAINS OVERVIEW

a problem. At present, the trailheads for Sven Slab and Gardener's Wall/ Tom's Thumb consist of small, rutted parking lots, but the preserve's master plan envisions a major trailhead development in the future. Currently the city is focusing on purchasing all of the land within the preserve's planning boundary, so there are limited funds for upgrading trailhead amenities. It may take many years before this trailhead receives a face-lift. In the meantime, the bumpy dirt access road helps preserve the quiet ambiance of this beautiful area, and the really important thing is that the cliffs and the surrounding Sonoran Desert are preserved for future generations.

As with any desert environment, beware of snakes and scorpions here. Staying on the trails preserves the desert ecosystem and helps you avoid being victimized by the thorny armor that virtually all desert plants have adopted for self defense.

The Sonoran Desert of the McDowell Mountains is alive with colorful blooms every spring.

MCDOWELL MOUNTAINS BETA

Drive time from Tucson ▲ 2 hours
Drive time from Phoenix ▲ 15–45 minutes
Drive time from Flagstaff ▲ 2¼ hours

Getting there: From Phoenix or Tucson, take the eastern Loop 101 freeway north through Scottsdale. (See the Pinnacle Peak map in the previous section.) Get off at exit 36 (Pima Road and Princess Drive). Go about 6 miles north on Pima Road to Dynamite Road and turn right (east). Head east on Dynamite (its name changes to Rio Verde Drive in the eastern section) 5 miles to 128th Street, which is a dirt road. Turn right on 128th Street and follow it south, as it gets bumpier and more rutted, for 3.2 miles to its dead end at Paraiso Road. There are no road signs marking Paraiso. It is handy to have a 4WD or high-clearance vehicle for the rutted portions of this drive. If your car can't negotiate some of the ruts, just park at a pullout and walk, as all vehicles can get within reasonable walking distance of the crags.

To reach Sven Slab, turn left (east) on Paraiso and follow it for just over half a mile of progressively rougher road to the obvious parking area near the base of the slabs. For Gardener's Wall and Tom's Thumb, turn right on Paraiso and follow it 0.2 mile. Turn left onto another dirt road here and follow it 0.4 mile, past a lone house, to its end at a small, rough parking lot. There are no garbage cans or restroom facilities at the trailheads, so please pack out your refuse.

From Flagstaff, take I-17 south to the Carefree Highway (exit 223). Follow the Carefree Highway 11.8 miles east to Scottsdale Road, where you turn right (south). Proceed 3.9 miles to Dynamite Road, where you turn left (east). After 2 miles on Dynamite you cross Pima Road. Continue traveling east on Dynamite Road and follow the directions above from there.

Approach: The approach to each rock is different, so details are listed separately for each section. Sven Slab approaches are 5–10 minutes. Gardener's Wall takes 30–45 minutes to access and Tom's Thumb requires about 50 minutes.

Season and Elevation: The rocks sit at 3000–4000 feet on the north slopes of the McDowell Mountains. Climbing is best here during the fall, winter, and spring. This is a great winter climbing area, but even here it can get chilly, sometimes making climbing uncomfortable on this shady side of the mountain. Summer temperatures routinely soar way above 100 degrees F, but it is still possible on many days to sneak in a morning climb or two before the sun reaches these north faces.

Regulations: All routes are in the McDowell Sonoran Preserve, owned by the City of Scottsdale. The city manages the preserve for environmental protection and passive recreation. Climbing is an approved recreational activity, but all visitors are required to remain on established trails. Given the abundant spiny desert vegetation, you will be happy you stayed on the trail anyway! No fires are permitted, and it is illegal to collect any plants, rocks, or artifacts. For information on the preserve, log on to *www.ci.scottsdale.az.us/preserve* or call (480) 312-7722.

Camping: No camping is allowed in the preserve. The nearest campground is Needle Rock in the Tonto National Forest. From the junction of Dynamite and Pima Roads, travel 14 miles east on Dynamite/Rio Verde Road to its dead end at Forest Road 20. Turn left (north) and follow this road 3 miles to the campground, which consists of dispersed sites. The campground is located at 1600 feet on the banks of the perennially flowing Verde River. There are picnic tables and trash cans, but no drinking water. Tent and RV camping is available at the McDowell Mountain Regional Park, a short distance away. It has hookups, water, and toilets. Follow Rio Verde Road to its end, turn right, and pass through the small town of Rio Verde to McDowell Mountain Road, which passes by the park entrance. If you would prefer to stay in a hotel, there are plenty of choices in Scottsdale within 10 miles of the crags.

Food and Supplies: All services are available in Scottsdale.

Gear: A standard rack will suffice for most routes here. A double set of cams come in handy on the longer routes, especially the Tom's Thumb cracks. Two ropes are needed to rappel off Gardener's Wall, and a 55-meter rope or 2 ropes are necessary for the Sven Slab and Tom's Thumb rappels. Phoenix and its suburbs have a number of gear stores.

Emergency Services: The closest hospital is the Mayo Clinic Hospital in Scottsdale at 5777 E. Mayo Boulevard, a short distance south of the Loop 101 highway at 56th Street. (480-515-6296)

Kids and Dogs: The Sven Slab area has a mild approach that is easily negotiated by children and dogs. Kids will have a tougher time with the steep approach hikes to Gardener's Wall and Tom's Thumb, but they will have a blast exploring the caves below Gardener's Wall, formed by huge boulders that tumbled off the wall and lodged in the narrow wash below. Dogs are allowed in the McDowell Sonoran Preserve, but they must be on a leash at all times.

Sven Slab

A trail angles up and left from the parking area, traversing below a series of small crags to Sven Slab, which is the obvious large, smooth slab. Routes 3–7 are on this main slab and take about 5 minutes to reach. A single large eyebolt at the top of the slab provides a convenient rappel and allows you to top-rope any of these climbs after leading one. The 90-foot rappel requires a 55-meter rope or double ropes. If you want to top-rope them all, bring a 60-meter rope to accommodate the extra length needed to place directional anchors on routes 3 and 4. Routes 1 and 2 are up around the corner to the left of this main slab, requiring a bit more exertion and an extra 5–8 minutes to reach. Most of the slab routes here are protected by bolts that are spaced much farther apart than most modern climbers are used to. If you are leading, be prepared to run it out. Fortunately, though, unlike Gardener's Wall, most of the original bolts here have been replaced with modern hardware.

Jamming the elegant thin crack of One For the Road *at Sven Slab*

LEFT-SIDE ROUTES

1. ONE FOR THE ROAD 5.6 ★★★

FA: Ted Olsen or Bob Puryear 1981 (both have claimed separate 1981 first ascents)

This beautiful route tackles the prominent, right-leaning thin crack that splits the clean face on the far left end of the wall. **Pitch One:** Ascend this gorgeous crack to a belay on a large ledge with a tree. The crack swallows small- to medium-sized cams and stoppers. This pitch is the main event and it is easy to walk off to the left and scramble down third-class slabs from its top. 130 feet. **Pitch Two:** Although this pitch isn't nearly as good as pitch one, it is still fun and milks a little more mileage out of the face. Move right from the belay ledge into the chimney on the right side of the wall. After about 15 feet, step left onto a ledge. Look for a bolt on the face above the left side of this ledge. Ascend the face past the bolt and discontinuous cracks that take stoppers, RPs, and small cams to the top. **Descent:** Scramble off on third-class ground to climber's left.

2. THE CHUTE 5.4 ★★

This is a very pleasant climb on a clean slab 50 feet right of *One for the Road*. This slab forms the skyline when viewed from the base of that

climb. Begin at a block on the left side of the slab. Move up and right to a bolt, then up the slab past a second bolt. A large cam fits the horizontal crack above, then a final bolt protects the upper face. Belay on the continuation of the ledge system that forms the top of *One for the Road*'s first pitch. Medium and large cams are useful for establishing this belay. The easiest descent is to traverse left on this ledge system past the *One for the Road* belay and descend as for that route.

RIGHT-SIDE ROUTES

To descend from all right-side routes, rappel 90 feet from an eye bolt at the top of the routes.

3. BLACK DEATH 5.8 ★
FA: Bob Puryear, Larry Braten 1985

This is the leftmost route on the main slab. Begin at a right-arching crack 20 feet left of *Cakewalk*. Ascend the crack to a stance where you

Kate McEwen powers up the initial moves of Black Death *at Sven Slab.*

can step up and left onto the face with a bolt. Taller folks can reach this bolt for their first piece; if you are shorter you will probably want to place a small to medium cam in the crack first. A fingertip lieback off the flake near the bolt helps you ascend the face to a second bolt. From there move straight up the face to another right-angling crack that leads to the eyebolt belay anchor. This crack takes stoppers low and #3 and #4 Camalots above. If you top-rope this climb, set a #3 Camalot in the crack directly above the bolts for a directional anchor. 2 bolts, gear, 110 feet.

4. CAKEWALK 5.8 ★
FA: Dan Dingle, Alex McGuffie 1978

Move up the face off the top of the large boulder 10 feet left of the flat, treed area where the trail meets the rock face. The crux of the route comes down low, between the first and second bolts. You can get a stopper in a flake above the second bolt. Move up and right past 2 more bolts to the eyebolt top anchor or move left above the flake to a third bolt, then up to the right-leaning wide crack mentioned in *Black Death*. Ascend this crack to the top eyebolt. If you top-rope this route it is a good idea to put quickdraws on some of the bolts for directionals. 4 bolts, 100 feet.

5. EGO TRIP 5.7 R or TR ★★

FA: Rick Hlava, Calvin Hahn 1985

This route begins either just left of or from the top of a small boulder in the tree-covered flat area where the trail first reaches the wall. A crux start leads up to a bolt, then continues up the face to a second bolt. Use care clipping this second bolt, as there is ground-fall potential here. Move up to an undercling off a flake that takes small to medium cams, then deal with a long runout from there to the third bolt on easier ground. Continue up to the eyebolt. 3 bolts, gear, 90 feet.

6. I SINKSO 5.8 R or TR ★

Begin this route 10 feet right of *Ego Trip* on the smooth right side of the face, just left of a boulder that sits next to the wall. The crux comes just above the ground on the way to the high first bolt. This is easier if you come at it from the right. There are some friable flakes to contend

with near this first bolt. Move up to a second bolt, then do a long runout on easier ground to a third bolt located up and right from the undercling flake on *Ego Trip*. From here head up and left to the eyebolt. Technically, the route stays right of the third bolt on *Ego Trip*, making for a very long runout at the top. In practice, the line is just as natural going up and left to clip the *Ego Trip* bolt, making the top less runout. 3 bolts, 90 feet.

7. QUAKER OATS 5.5 ★★★

FA: Stan Mish, Terry Price 1976

This is the best route on the main Sven Slab wall. To reach it go up the slope on the right side of the wall about 15 feet to where it is easy to step left onto the wall at a ledge. The first bolt is directly above the ledge. Continue up the face past 4 more bolts, then angle

Clean slab climbing is the name of the game on Sven Slab's Ego Trip.

Kate McEwen is lost in a sea of granite on Quaker Oats.

left to the eyebolt at the top. Most of this route is well protected but there is a runout on moderate ground between the fifth bolt and the eyebolt. 90 feet. **Variation**: If you want to squeeze a bit more climbing out of this route, continue up the slab above the eyebolt past 2 bolts to a single-bolt belay anchor where the angle eases. 40 feet. *Alternatively*, you can do a fun right-angling crack that is hard to see from the belay but begins on the left, turning a small roof. Either way, from the top you must scramble off or rappel from a single bolt. It is questionable whether the short bit of extra climbing is worth the hassle. 5 bolts (8 if you climb pitch two).

Gardener's Wall

From the parking area, walk up the wash for about 5 minutes to the first large boulders lying in it. At this point hunt for a good trail that climbs up the slope among the boulders on the left (east) side of the wash. Take the time necessary to find this trail; you'll be glad you did. After climbing a short way out of the wash, the trail parallels it, wandering up and down to avoid boulders. After about 15 minutes the trail approaches a section of wash choked with enormous boulders. A prominent spur trail leads right, into a series of caves covered with graffiti. Continue on the left fork of the trail to a point just above the pile of enormous boulders. Another spur branches right here. Take this fork and descend to the wash. There is often a cairn on the wash's far (west) side that helps mark this cutoff. Cross the wash by hopping over some large boulders and catch the trail on the far side at the cairn. An easy-to-follow trail leads up the steep slope to the base of the wall. It winds in and out of caves made by more fallen boulders as it approaches the climbing wall. These caves offer welcome shade during hot weather. The approach trail reaches the wall at the big flake that marks the start of *Hanging Gardens*. The total approach time is 25–35 minutes.

From the upper ridges of the McDowell Mountains, Pinnacle Peak is visible across the rising sea of houses.

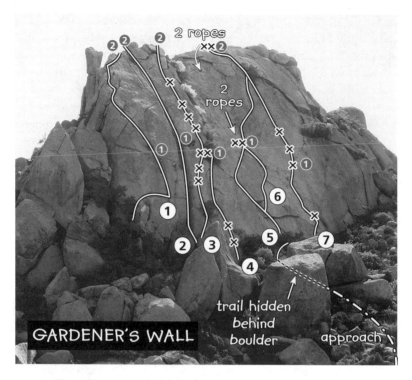

GARDENER'S WALL

trail hidden behind boulder

approach

1. THE PHANTOM 5.7 ★★

The crack on the first pitch is beautiful. Begin about 15 feet left of *Kreuser's Chimney*. To reach the base of the crack you need to scramble (fourth class) up the left side of a boulder pile that lies against the wall. **Pitch One:** Climb the left-trending thin crack up to a large ledge. 5.7, 70 feet. **Pitch Two:** Easier climbing up cracks and flakes that trend left above the belay leads to the summit ridge, where you can move right to a belay. 5.6, 120 feet. **Descent:** Continue traversing the summit ridge right to the double-rope rappel at the top of *Hanging Gardens*. **Variation:** An alternative to pitch two is to climb the face directly above the belay past two bolts and a right-leaning crack to the runout face above. This is the second pitch of *Phantom of the Opera*. 5.7 R.

2. KREUSER'S CHIMNEY DIRECT 5.3 ★

FA: Pitch One: Tom Kreuser, Dave Olson 1965; Pitch Two: Bruce Grubbs, Larry Treiber, Bill Sewrey 1977

This route tackles the obvious chimney on the left side of the face. **Pitch One:** Climb the chimney to a hole that you can squeeze through to reach a belay ledge on the right. 5.3, 100 feet. **Pitch Two:** Move back left into the chimney and follow it as it narrows into an off-width crack. 5.3, 100 feet. Bring lots of large nuts and cams. **Descent:** Traverse right along the summit ridge to reach the double-rope rappel station at the top of *Hanging Gardens.*

3. PARENTAL GUIDANCE 5.9 ★
FA: Jim Zahn, Chuck Hill, Jason Sands 1984
This route begins about 20 feet left of *Renaissance Direct* at a right-leaning crack to a face with 2 old, rusty bolts. Finish at the first belay station of *Renaissance Direct.* You can easily top-rope this climb from the first anchor on that climb.

4. RENAISSANCE DIRECT 5.7 ★★★
FA: Pitch One: Larry Treiber, Bruce Grubbs, Bill Sewrey 1977; Pitch Two: Chuck Hill, Eric Johnson 1983
This is one of the best climbs on the wall. It is located about 70 feet down and left from *Hanging Gardens*, where the trail first reaches the wall. The route is recognized by its short right-facing dihedral halfway up pitch one. **Pitch One:** Begin on the right edge of a steep slab and move past 2 old bolts (5.7) to the base of the dihedral. Ascend the dihedral, moving over a small roof (5.6) via fun hand jams. Traverse left at the top of the crack to a belay ledge with 2 good bolts next to a juniper. 2 bolts,

Stylish local climbers, like this lizard, will occasionally pose for photos.

100 feet. **Pitch Two:** Ascend the lovely face past 4 old bolts to the top. Small cams protect the ground between the third and fourth bolts, and a couple of medium to large cams (up to a #4 Camalot) are useful for protecting the easier moves near the top. The pitch finishes at the top of the rock. 5.7, 150 feet, 4 bolts, gear. **Descent:** Scramble 50 feet right to the double-rope rappel off of *Hanging Gardens*.

5. HANGING GARDENS 5.5 ★★★

FA: Lance Daugherty, Dane Daugherty, Larry Treiber, Joe Theobald 1965; FFA: Joe Theobald, Glen Kappel, Jon Biemer 1971

This is likely the finest 5.5 climb in Arizona. It is a perfect location for a first lead on natural gear or for an introduction to the pleasures of crack climbing. The approach trail reaches the rock at the base of this route, which is distinguished by the huge, right-facing flake that forms its first couple of moves. **Pitch One:** Climb up easy cracks to the base of the huge flake. A horizontal crack leads out onto the face left of the flake. A fun hand traverse along this crack leads to a small stance at the base of a long, right-leaning crack. This crack is sheer joy, and it swallows perfect protection, especially medium-sized Camalots. Belay at a small stance with a double-bolt anchor at crack's end above the top of the flake. 5.5, 125 feet. **Pitch Two:** The right-leaning crack reestablishes itself about 8 feet above the belay stance. It starts off as a shallow seam that takes stoppers and soon widens into a wonderful hand crack. Follow this to a brushy ledge, then step left and up to a double-bolt belay at the top of the rock. This pitch takes small to medium Camalots. 5.5, 155 feet. **Descent:** Descend via two double-rope rappels. The upper rappel, 110 feet, is from 2 good bolts, but the anchor lacks chains. Bring slings and rappel rings to back up whatever exists on the bolts. The lower rappel, 100 feet, utilizes new, wide-radius Metolius bolts through which you can thread the rope. You can set up a top rope for *Bruisin' and Cruisin'* from this rappel anchor.

6. BRUISIN' AND CRUISIN' 5.8 R or 5.8 TR ★★

FA: Pete Noebels, Dennis Abbink, Larry Treiber 1975

This giant flake makes for a beautiful top rope or a strenuous, scary lead. The route can be easily top-roped from the first belay on *Hanging Gardens*, but if you plan to lead it, bring a fist full of tube chocks or Big Bros. Get your arms rested and blast up the flake in an exquisite lieback. Leaders can duck into the slot from time to time to place pro. From the top of the flake either continue up *Hanging Gardens* or rappel off the anchor on that route using 2 ropes. 100 feet.

7. LICKETY SPLIT 5.7 R ★
FA: Larry Treiber, Dave Hodson 1975

This is a fun but runout and serious face climb that begins 30 feet right of *Hanging Gardens* at a short, right-angling crack. **Pitch One:** Climb up the crack toward the right until it is possible to cut back left, past a bolt, along a thin crack toward the right edge of a small overhang. Climb up the face for 25 feet with dubious protection to a single-bolt belay stance in a shallow scoop. 5.7 R, 70 feet. **Pitch Two:** Move up the face to a bolt, then up and right to a second bolt, which lies at the base of a water groove. Climb the groove with no protection to a brushy crack. Climb the crack until it joins the top of *Hanging Gardens* and belay from the double-bolt anchor. Rappel with 2 ropes as for *Hanging Gardens*. Bring RPs and Aliens in addition to a standard rack of stoppers and small to medium cams. 160 feet.

Tom's Thumb

Tom's Thumb stands proudly atop the ridge above the parking lot, beckoning climbers. There are two approach trails to the Thumb. One tackles the steep, nasty slope below the Thumb. While this is the quickest approach, it is also the least pleasant and the most environmentally damaging. Instead, use the more pleasant approach that follows the main wash past Gardener's Wall. From the parking area, follow the approach directions listed for Gardener's Wall to the point where the Gardener's Wall approach cuts off the main trail to cross the wash. For Tom's Thumb, continue up the main trail at this point for just a few more minutes of walking, till you reach an unusually large boulder with a pointy, triangular top that stands just right of the main trail. At this point you will be slightly south of Gardener's Wall. Turn right (west) on the spur trail that lies immediately past the pointy boulder. This trail leads you down into the wash, which you cross by scrambling over boulders. A good trail heads up the slope on the west side of the wash; it pays to find it rather than fighting your way through the thorny vegetation. This trail passes behind (south of) Gardener's Wall, running along the pleasant, open ridge up to the Thumb. The approach takes about 50 minutes.

The Thumb is encircled by routes, so this is a great place to follow the sun or the shade depending on the weather conditions. You reach the crag at its east face, and the first route you encounter is *Treiber's Deception*. Routes are described as you move counterclockwise around the formation from it. Routes 2 – 4 lie on nearby crags that are accessed by descending the slope to the south (left) from the Thumb's east face.

Descent: The descent for all routes on the Thumb itself is to rappel 90 feet from a triple-bolt anchor located on the far west end of the summit. Bring a single 55-meter rope or 2 ropes. The rappel bolts are big and new, but they don't have rappel chains on them. Bring a long piece of webbing to replace any old webbing that remains on this anchor. A trail encircles the crag, facilitating your return to the base of the route.

1. TREIBER'S DECEPTION 5.7 ★★★

FA: Larry Treiber, Becky Treiber, Bill Sewrey, Tom Kreuser 1967
FFA: Lance Dougherty, Dane Dougherty, Larry Treiber 1968

This fine route tackles the crack system that lies on the far left side of the east face. Begin by chimneying between a large boulder and the face to reach the base of the crack. Set protection and step onto the main wall. Ascend the crack as it widens, passing a block, to its end. Step left

Bridging the initial moves of Treiber's Deception

around the corner to an old, rusty bolt on the face. Climb the face past the bolt to a second bolt at the base of a wide crack. Climb this crack and step left at its top to a second wide crack that takes you to the top. Bring a standard rack augmented by large cams up to a #4 Camalot. 140 feet.

2. WATER DRAWN FROM AN ANCIENT WELL 5.7 ★

FA: Paul Paonessa, Kevin Stevens 1986

This is a pleasant but short climb that lies on the south face of the rock pile that lies 30 yards south of *Treiber's Deception*. It ascends the obvious thin cracks that lead to a left-angling hand crack. It finishes up a short, vertical crack to the summit. Walk off the back side, toward Tom's Thumb. 30 feet.

3. BARBEQUE CHIPS AND BEER 5.7 ★

There are some really enjoyable moves on this route, but a few changes have rendered it less pleasant than it once was. Begin about 40 feet left of *Slip N' Slide* beneath a line of 4 silver bolts. A mesquite tree has grown across the route between the first and second bolt, accounting for some of the degraded quality. Tackle the initial headwall via a thin crack that takes good stoppers and move up the face past the first bolt. Veer right to avoid the mesquite and then back left to clip the second bolt. From there continue unimpeded up the rest of the slab past 2 more bolts to the top. The final bolt's hanger has somehow been bent enough that it no longer accepts carabiners. Bring a loop of webbing to thread through the hanger, or better yet, top-rope this route after climbing *Slip N' Slide*. Walk off the rock to the east. 110 feet.

4. SLIP N' SLIDE 5.5 ★★
FA: Glen Dickinson, Dan Loden 1980

This is a very enjoyable slab climb that ascends the southwest face of a formation about 150 yards south of Tom's Thumb. The slab itself isn't visible from the base of the Thumb, but the boulder pile that forms its summit is. The easiest approach is to head down a trail that wends its way down the hill to the south, through large boulders, from the wide, flat area that lies just east of Tom's Thumb. This trail passes east of the boulders that form the slab's summit. After about 200 yards on this trail, veer right (west) down the slope, passing the summit boulders on their left. The large slab soon comes into view on your right, and it is easily reached. *Slip N' Slide* ascends the obvious brown water streak up the center of the slab past 3 rusty bolts. Bring a few stoppers and cams to augment the protection and to construct the top anchor. It is runout above the last bolt, but the difficulty eases. To descend, walk off the back (east) side of the rock. 100 feet.

Chance Traub grapples with the initial dihedral on Sacred Datura Direct.

5. SACRED DATURA DIRECT 5.9 ★★★
FA: Jim Waugh, John Ficker 1980

This is a gem! It will keep you continuously engaged throughout its entire 140 feet. It lies on the left side of the northeast face and begins by climbing a shallow dihedral that ends at a bolt 30 feet up the wall. A bolted arête lies 10 feet to the left and a wide crack lies 10 feet to the right of this shallow dihedral. Ascend the dihedral to the bolt (good gear placements can back up this rusty old bolt) and step around the corner to the right to gain a crack. Ascend this crack, past a fixed pin, to an alcove. Climb the discontinuous thin cracks above the alcove to a horizontal crack. A hangerless bolt protects the face above the horizontal. It has a head, so you can sling it with a small wired nut. Move up the face to a right-angling thin crack that takes gear. From there, either head up the fun but runout face directly above or, for better protection, move right to a wide crack finish. Save some gear for the top belay anchor. Walk west along the summit to the triple-bolt rappel anchor. This long, continuous

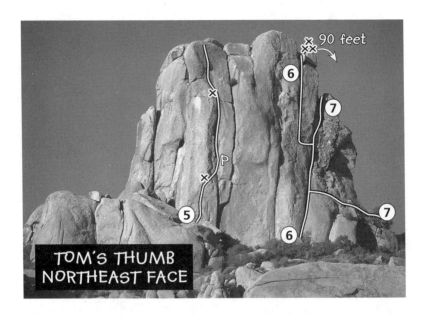

TOM'S THUMB
NORTHEAST FACE

pitch swallows a lot of small- to medium-sized gear. RPs and Aliens offer great protection for the initial shallow dihedral. In addition, bring doubles of #½ and #¾ Camalots and a standard rack with wired stoppers and up through a #2 Camalot.

6. GARBANZO BEAN 5.7 ★★

FA: Larry Treiber, Chuck Graf, Bob Watts, Phil Martineau

This route begins in the rightmost crack on the main northeast face and moves left to finish in another crack that begins 70 feet up the wall. A line of bolts (*Garbanzo Bean Direct*, 5.10+) runs up the wall 4 feet left of the initial crack to reach the base of the upper crack. Ascend the initial crack, which widens from hands to off-width, for 60 feet to a red ledge that allows a rightward escape off the face (this is the beginning of *Kreuser's Route*). Continue another 10 feet up the red chimney above, then move left onto the face at an obvious weakness covered with guano to reach the base of the upper crack. This traverse is the crux. Once on the face there is protection, but a fall on the initial move would send you swinging back into the chimney. You can minimize the swing by placing good protection high in the chimney, but this will lead to heinous rope drag as you climb the upper crack. Using double-rope technique will minimize this drag. Once established in the upper crack, ascend it to the top. It widens from thin hands to off-width. Belay from the triple-bolt rappel anchor. It helps to bring a double set of #1 to #4 Camalots in addition to a standard rack. 140 feet.

7. KREUSER'S ROUTE 5.4 ★
FA: Tom Kreuser, Don Weaver 1965

This route has a mountaineering feel. It begins at a third-class ledge on the northwest corner of the rock that traverses left (east) to join *Garbanzo Bean* 60 feet up. **Pitch One:** From the left end of the ledge the route ascends the chimney above, continuing up the chimney where *Garbanzo Bean* veers

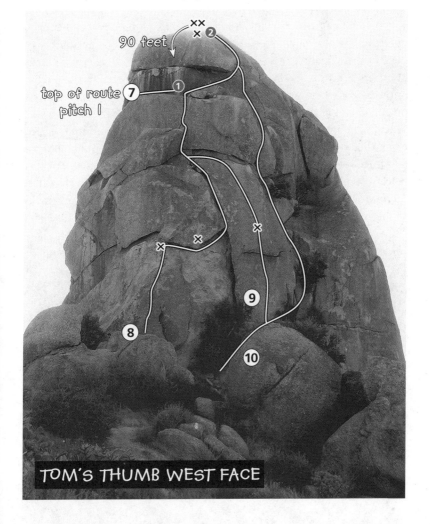

TOM'S THUMB WEST FACE

left onto the face. Belay on the huge ledge at the top of the chimney. You will need some big cams for this pitch, #4 Camalot and bigger. 5.4, 60 feet. **Pitch Two:** Move right (south) along the ledge until you can round the right side of the headwall above. Climb up cracks from here to the summit and belay from the triple-bolt rappel anchor. This is the top of *West Corner*. 5.0, 50 feet. **Variation:** There is a 5.6 direct start to pitch one that ascends the short, wide crack 10 feet right of *Garbanzo Bean*.

8. THE SETTLEMENT 5.7 ★
FA: Larry Treiber, Bill Sewrey, Don Witt 1967
FFA: Larry Treiber, Barbara Zinn 1974

This is an enjoyable route, but you have to contend with gritty rock near the bottom. Begin in the center of the west face at a small gray flake leaning against the wall. **Pitch One:** Climb the flake to a short, blunt arête. Clip a rusty bolt at the top of the arête and traverse right on gritty rock below an overhanging flake. A second old bolt, located on the flake, protects this traverse, but it can be backed up using cams in cracks behind the flake. At the end of the traverse climb up the nice crack that shoots through the right side of the crux overhang and up to a huge ledge beneath a headwall. Tackle the headwall via an obvious crack system to reach another large ledge and belay. 5.7, 70 feet. **Pitch Two:** Move right to circumvent a final headwall and cut left up cracks to the summit and a belay from the triple-bolt rappel anchor. This is the

An undercling traverse leads to a beautiful roof crack on The Settlement.

top of *West Corner*. You can easily do this route in a single pitch if you take precautions against rope drag. 5.0, 50 feet.

9. FACE FIRST 5.9 R or TR ★★
FA: Jason Sands, John Ficker 1985

I can't recommend this scary lead, but it makes for a fun top rope that is easy to set up off the triple-bolt rappel anchor. To avoid big swings, clip a directional runner into this route's 1 bolt and use a cam or stopper for a second directional along the big ledge above the bolt. This route ascends the steep, smooth face immediately right of the crux overhang on *The Settlement*. Begin by scrambling up an easy ramp (the beginning of *West Corner*) to a ledge below the face. Climb the steep face on small, delicate holds to a horizontal crack. Delicately move up past the horizontal to the bolt on the face. The climbing eases above the bolt. Join *The Settlement* at the large ledge below the headwall. If you do want to lead it, bring a couple of medium-sized nuts or cams to place in the horizontal. 50 feet.

10. WEST CORNER 5.1 ★
FA: Dick Hart, Bill McMorris 1948

This enjoyable meander has traditionally been rated fourth class, but it feels more difficult than that. Begin about 20 feet right of *The Settlement*. Climb a right-leaning ramp past a tree for 20 feet. From here cut left and up into a double set of wide cracks (instead of continuing up the obvious low-angled face directly in front of you). Follow these wide cracks up to the second big ledge on *The Settlement* and step around the right side of the headwall above to gain the summit via wide cracks. Bring a small rack with gear up to a #4 Camalot. You can break the climb into two pitches. 110 feet.

Matt Moss puzzles out the sequence on Face First.

Granite Mountain

Granite Mountain is Arizona's premier multi-pitch traditional crag. It is located just outside Prescott in the cool pine woodlands of the Prescott National Forest, and it is the centerpiece of a designated wilderness area. So many outstanding crack and face climbs adorn its walls that *Mountain Magazine* named it one of North America's ten best crags. Its soaring walls are exquisitely textured, offering one wonderful crack climb after another. Plenty of excellent steep face and slab climbing also exists here. If you are a visiting traditional climber, you don't want to leave Granite Mountain off of your itinerary.

"The Mountain," as it is referred to by Prescott climbers, hosts some of the longest routes in this guide, at up to five pitches. The Swamp Slabs section of the cliff offers shorter routes that provide a good introduction to the climbing. Granite Mountain was a favorite destination for the Syndicato Granitica climbing fraternity during the 1970s, making it one of the most historic climbing areas in Arizona. This band of irreverent and highly skilled climbers left an indelible mark on Arizona climbing and scores of classic climbs in their wake. In keeping with the fashion of the time, these climbers tended to underrate their routes; the worst indignity one could imagine would be to have one's route downgraded on a subsequent ascent. In the intervening years, nobody has seen fit

A climber stems the beautiful square slot on the first pitch of Magnolia Thunder Pussy.

155

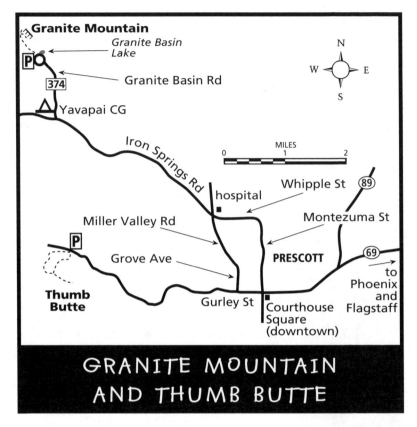

GRANITE MOUNTAIN AND THUMB BUTTE

to recalibrate those original, conservative ratings to achieve consistency with those from more recently developed areas. Because of that, ratings here tend to be stiffer than at some of the other crags in this book. More than one climber has returned from his or her first Granite Mountain trip waxing poetic about the quality of the climbing in one breath and bemoaning the fact that they felt sandbagged by the ratings in the next. Especially when you get up around 5.9 you will probably feel as if these routes serve up more than you have come to expect at the grade. None of the Granite Mountain ratings are unreasonable, but this is a place where it is wise to introduce yourself to the area at a more modest grade than you ordinarily do.

Both Granite Mountain and Thumb Butte, the neighboring climbing area, are closed to climbing from approximately February 1 through July 15 each year to protect nesting peregrine falcons. This encompasses the entire nesting period, from courtship in early spring through the fledging of the young in midsummer. Thanks to the efforts of many conservationists and the respect of hikers and climbers, the peregrine falcon is no longer on the endangered species list. This does not mean that they no longer need our protection, but rather that the protection efforts have been successful. Please respect the stated closures for the sake of the peregrines, as well as for the sake of future relations between climbers and the Prescott National Forest.

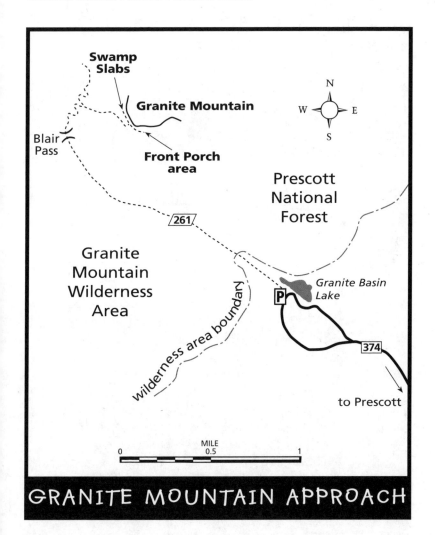

GRANITE MOUNTAIN APPROACH

Swamp Slabs

Front Porch area

Flying Buttress

approach

GRANITE MOUNTAIN OVERVIEW

GRANITE MOUNTAIN BETA

Drive time from Tucson ▲ 3½ hours

Drive time from Phoenix ▲ 1½ hours

Drive time from Flagstaff ▲ 1½ hours

Getting there: Prescott lies 95 miles northwest of Phoenix and 95 miles southwest of Flagstaff. From the south, drive north on I-17 to SR 69 (exit 262). This highway leads directly to Prescott. From the north, drive south on I-17 to exit 278, marked Highway 169 and Cherry Road. Follow SR 169 southwest to the junction with SR 69 and turn right.

From either direction, once you are on SR 69, follow it north and west to Prescott. In town there is a prominent junction with SR 89. Stay in the left lane at this junction and follow signs to Gurley Street. Follow Gurley to Courthouse Square, the center of historic downtown Prescott, and turn right on Montezuma. After making two sweeping turns, Montezuma turns into Iron Springs Road. Follow this road out of town. At milepost 3 turn right on Granite Basin Road (Forest Road 374). Follow this paved road for another 3.6 miles and turn right into the Playa parking lot immediately after passing the lake.

Approach: From the trailhead, the rock is a 1.5-hour, steep uphill hike. The specific approach information for each portion of the cliff is listed in its respective section.

Season and Elevation: Granite Mountain is at 6500 feet and is suitable for year-round climbing. It can be chilly in the winter, but the south or west-facing aspect of most routes provides lots of winter sun. Watch for severe afternoon thunderstorms in July and August. See the next paragraph for the seasonal closures.

Regulations: The cliff is closed for peregrine falcon nesting each year from approximately February through July. Contact the Prescott National Forest at 344 South Cortez St., Prescott, AZ 86303, (928) 443-8000, TTY (928) 443-8001 or *www.fs.fed.us/r3/prescott* for exact closure information. There is a $2-per-vehicle fee to park in the Granite Basin Recreation Area (Wednesdays are free). Golden Eagle and Golden Access passes are accepted in lieu of this fee. The gate into the access road doesn't open until sunrise.

Camping: Camping with water and outhouse facilities is available at the Yavapai Campground, which you pass on Forest Road 374. Free car camping is allowed at designated sites in the Prescott National Forest, but there are no such sites near Granite Mountain. See the Thumb Butte chapter for locations up Thumb Butte Road. Primitive, free camping is permitted 200 feet away from trails and water sources in the Granite Mountain Wilderness area, which begins at a fence approximately 0.5 mile into the hike toward the mountain. Don't expect water past the parking lot.

Food and Supplies: Water is available in the parking lot. Take plenty with you on the long hike to the cliff. Prescott is a 15-minute drive and hosts a wide range of restaurants and supermarkets. Prescott also has a gear shop, as well as numerous hotels and motels for those who prefer not to camp.

Gear: A standard to large rack is necessary for these long, traditional routes. Doubles of camming devices are useful on many routes. It is wise to bring some large cams for Granite Mountain's many wide cracks. Double ropes or a single 60-meter rope are needed for descents from climbs in the Front Porch area, but a standard 50-meter rope is sufficient for the Swamp Slabs area.

Emergency Services: A full-service hospital, Yavapai Regional Medical Center, is located at the corner of Iron Springs Road and Miller Valley Road: 1003 Willow Creek Road. (928-445-2700) Additionally, the sheriff's office maintains a backcountry search and rescue team. (928-771-3260) A rescue litter is stashed at the Front Porch.

Kids and Dogs: Although the Granite Mountain climbing area is not a good place for kids unless they're very sturdy hikers, the Granite Basin Recreation Area provides wonderful hiking and a small lake. Dogs are welcome on a leash in the wilderness area, but unless your dog is happy to wait for you while you disappear above for long periods of time, this may not be much fun for the dog or for neighboring climbers.

Swamp Slabs

The Swamp Slabs area contains the highest concentration of moderate routes at Granite Mountain. Many of the routes here are shorter than elsewhere on the mountain, and the descent is shorter and easier, making it a good destination for first-time Granite Mountain climbers. Although shorter, the climbs here are of extremely high quality, including some of the finest moderate, multi-pitch climbs in the state.

From the parking lot, follow Trail 261 west 1.5 miles to a trail junction with a gate at Blair Pass. The trail passes below the cliff, providing you with mouth-watering views of the climbing that is the payoff for your significant exertions on the approach. From Blair Pass, continue north (right) on Trail 261 (the trail is marked by a sign) toward the mountain. The trail climbs moderately here. About 10 minutes after departing the pass, you will arrive at the beginning of a series of switchbacks. At the third left switchback, which is identifiable by the large boulders (the first you will have come across), leave the main trail and follow an obscure climber's trail on your right. The beginning of this trail is strewn with boulders and sometimes is overgrown with prickly pear cactus, making it hard to spot. Don't be fooled into taking the more pronounced path leading off the main trail at the second left switchback, which has a large pine tree but no large boulders next to it. While this path looks good at first, it soon mires you in a nightmare of chaparral.

The climber's path meanders up and east. Although difficult to find at times, this trail is reasonably well-defined. If you find yourself thrashing through the bushes and feeling as though you are heading where no climber has ever gone before, stop, turn around, and find the trail again. You'll spare yourself many scratches and much frustration, as well as help curb the proliferation of trails to nowhere. After approximately 10 minutes of walking on the climber's trail, you'll reach some small orange granite slabs. The trail continues to angle east (right) for about

100 yards to a larger, lighter gray set of slabs below two pinyon pine trees. At this point, move left up the steep trail that leads to the Swamp Slabs (rather than contouring to the right over the granite slabs, which leads to the Front Porch area). After another 10 minutes of steep hiking, the trail reaches the base of the climbing cliff. Move left along the base of the cliff, up the steep gully, to a huge ponderosa pine. This tree lies on the left side of Pine Tree Ledge and is the staging area for all Swamp Slabs routes.

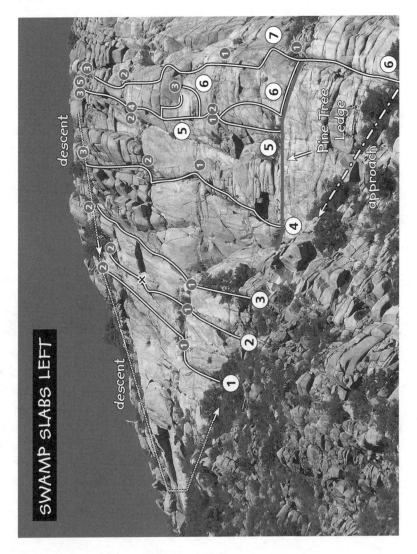

Descent: The descent for all Swamp Slabs area climbs is to scramble north (left) along the top of the buttress, past a huge alligator juniper, until you reach a low-angle slab. Carefully descend this slab, zigzagging across it to take advantage of several low-angle seams. From the bottom of the slab, work your way down the north edge of the Swamp Slabs to the large pine at the base. Use caution on this descent—it is exposed and slippery.

1. BEGINNER 5.4 ★★
FA: Rusty Baille, Prescott College students 1970

This short, enjoyable route begins at a prominent, left-facing dihedral at the extreme left side of the Swamp Slabs. It provides two distinctly different and equally enjoyable pitches. **Pitch One:** Lieback and jam the

Clean, elegant cracks abound at Granite Mountain. Climbers on Beginner. *(Photo: Chance Traub)*

crack in the back of the dihedral, using small footholds on the slippery but low-angle left face. Belay at a pile of blocks up and right from the top of the dihedral, below a series of flakes on the slab above. Wired stoppers and a selection of cams protect this pitch well. 5.4, 70 feet. **Variation:** A fun variation to this pitch is to climb the low-angle crack 10 feet right of the dihedral. **Pitch Two:** Move up the flake system and the discontinuous cracks to the clean face above. Although it looks from below as if protection might be sparse, many good nut placements exist in these cracks. Belay on the large ledge that forms the descent ramp. 5.4, 100 feet. **Variation:** An alternative to this second pitch is to move your belay 30 feet to the right and do the second pitch of *Debut*.

2. THE CRAWL 5.7 ★

FA: Rusty Baille, Jonathon Bjorklund, Kent Madin 1970

This route starts 30 feet right of *Beginner* and 40 feet left of *Debut*, below a right-leaning, right-facing dihedral. **Pitch One:** Climb up the dihedral and ascend the crack above to a large, bush-covered ledge and belay. 5.5, 80 feet. **Pitch Two:** Climb the right-facing flake above the ledge to a tiny roof. Turn the roof to the left and move into a right-leaning chimney, which forms the crux. Move past a bolt and turn another roof at the top of the chimney. Finish up a crack to the huge alligator juniper. 5.7, 100 feet.

3. DEBUT 5.5 ★★★

FA: Rusty Baille, David Lovejoy, Jack Hauck 1970

Along with *Hanging Gardens* at the McDowell Mountains, this route is in contention for the title of best 5.5 climb in Arizona. Begin below a shallow crack 10 feet left of the large pine on Pine Tree Ledge. The crack leads up to a prominent overhang. A standard Granite Mountain rack with lots of wired stoppers and a couple large cams works well here. **Pitch One:** Ascend the shallow cracks up to a roof in a pegmatite band. Haul yourself over the small roof on some buckets and ascend the double cracks above, which get progressively lower-angled and brushier. Run the rope out to a spacious belay at blocks on a large ledge. 5.4, 150 feet. **Pitch Two:** This is a beautiful pitch. Step across a gully to the right and face climb up a series of blocks, making good use of a series of mantle moves. From here move up into a gorgeous, shallow dihedral just to the right of a prominent roof. Delightful, continuous 5.5 climbing on clean rock up the well-protected dihedral deposits you on a large ledge immediately right of the gigantic alligator juniper on the descent. 5.5, 150 feet.

4. GREEN HORNS TO GREEN DAGGER 5.6 ★

FA: Green Horns—David Lovejoy, Steve Dieckhoff 1971; Green Dagger—Larry Treiber, Becky Treiber, Tom Taber, Joe Theobald

This route begins where Pine Tree Ledge narrows conspicuously, about 40 feet right of the pine tree. **Pitch One:** This is the first pitch of *Green Horns*. Follow the left-facing dihedral on the left side of a large flake up and right to a belay atop the flake. 5.6, 120 feet. **Pitches Two and Three:** *Green Horns* traverses left from here, but I recommend continuing up the upper two pitches of *Green Dagger*. The climbing on these pitches is easier than pitch one. From the ledge, continue up another left-facing dihedral, belay on another ledge, and then follow the crack to a short face to the summit. 200 feet.

5. DISLOCATION DIRECT 5.6 ★★★

FA: David Lovejoy, Jonathon Bjorklund, Kent Madin 1971

This classic crack climb is accessed by walking 100 feet right from the pine tree along Pine Tree Ledge. Locate the vertical crack that rises from a small grove of oak trees growing on the ledge. **Pitch One:** Follow the obvious crack and step right at its end onto a huge belay ledge. 5.6, 80 feet. **Pitch Two:** Ascend the right-facing corner above the belay. Step left at its top into a short, left-facing corner. At its top climb a small, right-facing corner with a flake/crack in it up to a small but comfortable belay ledge. 5.6, 120 feet. **Pitch Three:** Straight up cracks and blocks above the belay to the top of the cliff. 5.4, 120 feet.

6. DISLOCATION BUTTRESS 5.4 ★

FA: Larry Treiber, Becky Treiber 1969

This fun climb ascends a prominent, low-angle dihedral/gully that begins where the approach trail meets the cliff. Small to large nuts and cams are useful. **Pitch One:** Climb up the dihedral/gully to a belay by small trees on Pine Tree Ledge. The pitch ends at the start of *Tread Gently*. **Pitch Two:** Move the belay left 40 feet to the next group of trees, below a right-angling weakness in the slab above. This belay is about 10 feet right of the normal start to *Dislocation Direct*. Climb up right to a crack that heads left to a corner. Belay on the same huge ledge as the belay on top of *Dislocation Direct*'s first pitch. **Pitch Three:** Climb the initial dihedral of *Dislocation Direct*'s second pitch to the left side of a small roof. Traverse

Opposite: Nate Burk laying it back on the ultra-clean second pitch of Debut

Dislocation Direct *allows you to get above it all.*

out right onto the face along weaknesses above the roof and belay on a comfortable ledge. **Pitch Four:** Move left to reach a short, right-facing corner. Climb the corner to a horizontal crack where you traverse left to reach the flake/crack in the shallow corner described for pitch two of *Dislocation Direct*. Climb this flake/crack to a belay on the same ledge as *Dislocation Direct*'s second pitch. **Pitch Five:** Continue straight up cracks and blocks to the top of the cliff, the same as *Dislocation Direct*'s third pitch.

7. TREAD GENTLY 5.8- ★★
FA: Rusty Baille, solo, 1971
  Gentle treading is required on several sections of this beautiful route up the nose of the buttress, though the brief crux involves more strenuous hand

jamming around a small roof. The route begins at a small oak tree located where Pine Tree Ledge turns a sharp corner and becomes a ramp that slants more steeply down to the right. Bring a standard Granite Mountain rack with RPs, a #3 Camalot, and a #½ Tricam. **Pitch One:** A series of cracks and hollow flakes mark the initial moves of the route. Thoughtful nut work is needed to find solid rock for protecting these initial moves. The flakes lead up to a slanting crack, which you traverse left to an obvious flake that rests on the nose of the buttress. Step left and ascend the easy and fun crack that forms the flake's left side. Belay on a comfortable ledge at the top of the flake. 5.6, 80 feet. **Pitch Two:** Ascend the thin crack that splits the low-angle face above the belay ledge. Step left and ascend a nice hand crack that snakes around the right side of an obvious triangular roof. Turning the roof provides the awkward crux. Continue about 8 feet above the roof, then move left onto the exposed face at a series of incipient horizontal seams and a couple of knobs. This traverse can be done high (using the knobs for your feet) or low (using them for your hands). A #½ Tricam provides welcome protection when plugged into a conspicuous round pocket after you step onto the face. Ascend the face and a shallow, thin crack above the pocket to a belay ledge beneath a clean dihedral. Beware of rope drag on this long, wandering pitch, especially as you turn the crux roof and on the leftward traverse onto the face above. 5.8-, 150 feet. **Pitch Three:** Ascend the clean dihedral to easy scrambling up and left that ends at the top of the buttress. 5.2, 110 feet.

8. MAGICIAN 5.6 ★

FA: David Lovejoy, Jack Hauck, Jonathon Bjorklund, Dave Baker 1970

To reach this route, traverse right on Pine Tree Ledge around a nose to where the ledge becomes a slanting ramp that descends more steeply. Scramble down this steeper ramp, past one exposed section where some climbers may prefer to use a rope. Continue down the ramp about 100 feet beyond the exposed section until you are standing below a portion of the wall scored by a series of shallow, vertical grooves. Pitch one goes up these grooves. Bring a standard Granite Mountain rack, including RPs and a #3 Camalot. **Pitch One:** Ascend the shallow grooves to a brushy dihedral. Continue up the dihedral and step left to a belay on the ledge at its top. 5.6, 80 feet. **Pitch Two:** Step left from the belay and ascend a gorgeous hand crack for 30 feet to a brushy, left-facing corner. Step right at the top of the corner to a belay near a small tree on a ledge (Grand Traverse Ledge). 5.6, 80 feet. **Pitch Three:** Angle right up the low-angle

slab above the belay ledge (good RP placement) to the base of a left-facing dihedral. Ascend this enjoyable dihedral, which has a rightward jog about two-thirds of the way up, to a brushy ledge. There is a bit of a runout from the RP placement on the traverse to the first good nut in the dihedral. 5.6, 100 feet. **Pitch Four:** Fourth-class climbing up and left takes you to the top of the buttress.

9. HASSAYAMPA 5.8- ★★

FA: Karl Karlstrom, David Lovejoy 1971

This climb lacks an independent start and begins on the Grand Traverse Ledge. The standard and easiest way to reach it is to climb the first pitch of *Chim Chimney*, a somewhat mangy 5.6 chimney. Alternatively, you can reach Grand Traverse Ledge via *Magician, Magnolia Thunder Pussy*, or any of the other nearby climbs. Once you reach *Hassayampa*, get ready for some very enjoyable crack and chimney climbing. Bring a standard Granite Mountain rack with 1–2 cams in each size up to #4. **Pitch One:** The most efficient approach to *Hassayampa* is up the first pitch of *Chim Chimney*. There are some reasonably nice moves in this chimney, but the rock quality is not the greatest, so use caution. To reach it, follow the approach to *Magician* and continue traversing right on the downward-slanting ramp of Pine Tree Ledge for several hundred feet until you are nearly in the back of a prominent, deep alcove. An obvious, wide chimney/gully rises here. Pitch one ascends this chimney to its top on Grand Traverse Ledge. Traverse 30 feet right to a comfortable belay at the base of a large, left-facing dihedral. 5.6, 150 feet. *Note:* If you choose to approach *Hassayampa* via *Magician*, set up a belay at the top of *Magician*'s second pitch and then move right on Grand Traverse Ledge to *Hassayampa* in a separate pitch. **Pitch Two:** Now the fun begins! Tiptoe up the low-angle face that forms the left side of the left-facing dihedral, using the thin crack in the back of the dihedral for finger locks and good protection. The crack widens above into a wonderful hand crack and then widens still more to provide a brief, off-width crux. Above the crux the crack again narrows to hand size. Establish a comfortable belay in a hollow where the crack you have been ascending joins a chimney on the left (the second pitch of *Chim Chimney*). Some climbers may find this pitch challenging for the grade. 5.7+, 80 feet. **Pitch Three:** *Chim Chimney*'s third pitch moves left from this belay up another chimney. *Hassayampa*'s crux consists of a thin crack up a somewhat polished, low-angle slab directly above the belay to the right of that chimney. Above the crux slab you encounter easy climbing up a crack in a shallow dihedral that aims for the big roof directly above. You pass the roof by wiggling up a narrow chimney that passes through it. Keep chimneying up past the roof to a wider, much shallower chimney with several cracks in the back of it to a belay at the top of the buttress. 5.8-, 140 feet.

10. MAGNOLIA THUNDER PUSSY 5.9- ★★★

FA: David Lovejoy, Jack Hauck, Jonathon Bjorklund 1970
FFA: Karl Karlstrom, David Lovejoy, Scott Baxter 1971

This is one of the best climbs here, and it has achieved legendary status among Granite Mountain climbers. If you've always dreamed of climbing one of the famous Devil's Tower stemming slots but you haven't been able to make the trip to Wyoming, this is your climb. Come armed with a generous supply of Camalots up to #4, in addition to a standard Granite Mountain rack. Many climbers find this route to be stiff for its grade.

Approach as for *Hassayampa* but continue traversing right on Pine Tree Ledge another 80 feet beyond the prominent alcove to the base of a beautiful, unmistakable, square slot. This slot composes the stellar first pitch. **Pitch One:** This climb wastes no time getting down to business. After a short scramble up the left edge of a flake to a small ledge, it attacks the fine crack that forms the right side of the slot. After a few strenuous 5.9- hand jams, the left wall of the slot gets close enough for you to stem out to it for a little breather. Easier stemming and jamming conduct you up the slot to a small ledge that provides a welcome respite from your labors before you tackle the second crux at the roof above. The roof can be turned using either the left or the right crack. Both are rated 5.9-, but the left one is typically considered easier despite being more awkward. A short run up the cracks above lands you at a comfortable belay on top of several blocks. 5.9-, 80 feet. **Pitch Two:** Scramble up a pile of shattered blocks and veer right into an easy crack up to a belay on a comfortable ledge immediately below a low-angle, right-leaning crack that is capped by an overhanging flake. 5.2, 60 feet. **Pitch Three:** Ascend the crack to a stance below the overhanging flake. Chimney out the slot formed by the flake. A #4 Camalot is very useful for protecting this airy and frightening move. Make sure you use long slings below the flake to avoid rope drag after you turn the roof. Belay at a ledge about 20 feet above the flake/roof. 5.7, 100 feet. **Pitch Four:** Run for the top, up the obvious chimney above. The lower reaches of the chimney are an easy gully, but above the walls close in tighter and you tunnel your way through a deep, almost subterranean slot that calls for some nice chimney moves. You emerge from the chimney on the summit of the buttress. 5.5, 150 feet. **Descent:** Move left on second-class ground to join the standard Swamp Slabs descent. It is easy to end up going too high, so keep your eyes peeled for the large alligator juniper where the standard descent begins, which you reach after 300 feet of walking.

Front Porch Area

To get to the Front Porch, follow the approach directions to the Swamp Slabs above. At the large granite slab with two pinyon pines, veer right. The approach to the Swamp Slabs continues steeply uphill, but the Front Porch approach crosses the slabs and contours to the right well below

FRONT PORCH AREA
LEFT, VIEW I

Flying Buttress

standard route

Crack Lover's
Variation
Pitch 2

Reunion
Variation

Crack Lover's
Variation
Pitch I

the base of the rock. Take the time to find the faint but well-established trail. The path ends at a large, flat slab of granite, the Front Porch, at the base of the prominent Flying Buttress. This is a great staging area for all climbs on the main face of Granite Mountain.

Descent: The descent for Front Porch routes entails three rappels down *Coke Bottle*, which lies along the massive dihedral that forms the right side of the Flying Buttress. The first anchor is located up and left of the *High Exposure Exit* finish to *The Classic*. You need 2 ropes or a 60-meter rope for this first rappel. Two additional rappels from obvious double-bolt anchors land you on the ground.

1. COATIMUNDI WHITEOUT TO CANDYLAND, GRADE III 5.9 ★★★

FA: Coatimundi Whiteout—Scott Baxter, Jim Whitfield 1971
FFA of pitches one and two—Scott Baxter, Lee Dexter 1971
FA: Candyland—David Lovejoy, Dwight Bradley 1970
FFA—Karl Karlstrom, Rusty Baille, David Lovejoy 1972

This is one of Arizona's best and most memorable climbs. Don't miss it if you can climb sustained 5.9, but be forewarned that most climbers find this route hard for its grade. Begin at face moves below and left of a very obvious, left-facing dihedral. **Pitch One:** Climb through face and lieback moves to the huge dihedral. Ascend the dihedral to a double-bolt hanging belay. 5.8, 130 feet. **Pitch Two:** Climb the dihedral to a small ledge with a bolt above it. Climb up the large corner crack to an obvious 20-foot traverse left to a left-facing flake crack. Continue up the crack to a small roof before traversing right to a double-bolt belay on a ledge. Beware of rope drag. 5.8+, 130 feet. **Pitch Three:** Follow the short and easy ramp to the base of the Great Roof. 5.4, 40 feet. **Pitch Four:** You won't believe this thing could be climbed at 5.7, but it can. Hand traverse right below the roof past pitons and a bolt to an inspiring belay on the right side of the roof. 5.7, 60 feet. **Pitch Five:** Climb straight up the thin crack system past a small roof. Jam up and left to the right-angling crack that leads to the summit. 5.9-, 100 feet. **Descent:** Hike east to the *Coke Bottle* rappel.

2. THE CLASSIC 5.7 or 5.8 ★★★

FA: Scott Baxter, Karl Karlstrom, Lee Dexter 1968

This excellent route provides a moderate tour of the soaring central wall of Granite Mountain. It ascends the prominent dihedral system that forms the left side of the Flying Buttress. Several variations are possible for each pitch. The route protects nicely with a standard Granite Mountain rack that includes cams up to a #4. The standard first pitch begins in the low-angle dihedral that forms the left side of a large, semi-detached block. Two alternative starts, both highly recommended, begin about 50 feet to the right, where a clean face forms the left side of a prominent, left-facing dihedral. A wide but elegant flairing fist crack splits the center of this clean face. This is the excellent first pitch (5.8) of *Crack Lover's Variation*. The left-facing dihedral to the right is the enjoyable first pitch (5.7) of *Reunion Variation*.

Climbers on the exhilarating third pitch of The Classic

Pitch One: The standard first pitch ascends the low-angle dihedral about 40 feet to the point where the crack in the dihedral begins to get wide (this off-width crack is another option, called *Karl's Corner*, 5.9). Step right to a second crack here and ascend it to a belay at a tree on the higher of two spacious ledges. *Crack Lover's Variation* and *Reunion* alternative pitches both end at this same belay. 5.6, 80 feet. **Pitch Two:** The standard route ascends the 5.4 chimney straight above for 70 feet to a belay ledge at a tree. A much better alternative is to ascend the second pitch of *Crack Lover's Variation*, the beautiful hand crack that splits the face left of the chimney. 5.7 moves right off the belay lead to easier climbing up a wide, right-arching crack. The crack narrows again above the arch and provides a nice 5.8 finish up the main crack or a slightly easier alternative if you step left at the top. Either way you end up on an easy, right-leaning ramp that leads up to the belay at the top of the standard route's chimney. 5.7 or 5.8, 80 feet. **Pitch Three:** Ascend the V-shaped dihedral above the belay. Pass a small roof on the left and keep going up the dihedral to a second small roof. Leave the dihedral here to tackle a solitary crack that diagonals up and right through the roof and onto the airy face above. The crack offers easy (5.3) but exhilarating climbing up this face. Belay at a stance on the narrow fin that forms the top of the Flying Buttress. 120 feet, 5.7. Alternatively, you can continue up the

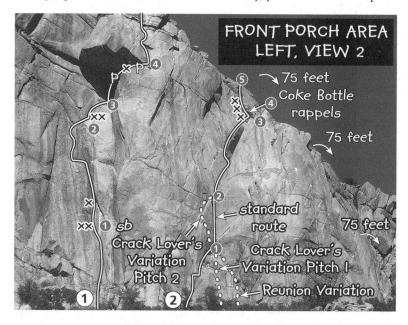

FRONT PORCH AREA LEFT, VIEW 2

75 feet
Coke Bottle rappels

75 feet

75 feet

standard route

Crack Lover's Variation Pitch 2

Crack Lover's Variation Pitch 1

Reunion Variation

sb

dihedral at the second roof to the belay described at the top of pitch four, but it is a lot more fun to do the route described here.

Once again, *The Classic* offers you a choice at this point. For those who have had enough climbing, or if the weather is threatening, you can scramble down to the *Coke Bottle* rappel station from here. Otherwise you can finish with the *High Exposure Exit*, which offers another good pitch of climbing. To descend from here, do a fourth-class scramble southwest 15 feet down from the belay atop pitch three and squeeze east through a hole to a short slab that ends at a wide ledge. Follow the ledge to its east end, where you will find the double bolts that form the anchor for the second of the three *Coke Bottle* rappels.

Pitch Four: If you choose to continue climbing, tiptoe along the narrow crest of the Flying Buttress, past a horn that can be slung for protection, to a belay where it meets the main wall. The first bolt of pitch five provides part of the anchor for this belay. 5.0, 40 feet. **Pitch Five:** This pitch is called the *High Exposure Exit*. Delicate, exposed face climbing leads up and right along two parallel seams past 3 bolts to a gully that you take up and left. 5.6+, 100 feet. **Descent:** Locate a double-bolt rappel anchor that forms the first of three rappels down the right (east) side of the Flying Buttress, down the *Coke Bottle* route.

3. GRANITE JUNGLE 5.7 or 5.9 ★★
FA: Larry and Becky Treiber 1970

Fun crack climbing characterizes this route. Climbing the first two pitches makes a fine 5.7 outing. Combine these with pitch two of *Chieu Hoi* for more challenge (5.9). This route begins at a flake crack in the center of the face that lies between the *Chieu Hoi* dihedral and another large, right-facing dihedral 50 feet to the left. Bring a standard Granite Mountain rack that includes cams up to a #4 Camalot. **Pitch One:** Ascend the flake and the crack above to a ledge that slopes down to the right. Move right 5 feet on this ledge to the base of another crack. Ascend this widening crack to its end on a large ledge covered with trees and cacti. 5.6, 120 feet. **Pitch Two:** Move the belay 10 feet left to the base of a clean crack that splits the face immediately right of a right-facing dihedral. Ascend the crack and the dihedral above to the comfortable belay ledge at the top of *Chieu Hoi*, pitch one. 5.7, 80 feet.

You have three choices at this point: (1) Continue on *Granite Jungle* up the claustrophobic off-width chimney above you to the left, 5.9+; (2) climb the second pitch of *Chieu Hoi*, 5.9; or (3) end your climb here, rappelling off as described for *Chieu Hoi*. The second option is recommended.

4. CHIEU HOI 5.7 or 5.9 ★★★
FA: Scott Baxter, Karl Karlstrom 1971

This is another outstanding route. You can rappel after pitch one to make the climb 5.7. This beautiful line ascends the prominent dihedral

that lies on the left edge of the large, white slab that forms the cliff's right side. It protects well using a standard Granite Mountain rack. **Pitch One:** Ascend the right-facing dihedral. The lower part is 5.4, and it becomes steeper and cleaner the higher you go. Belay on a spacious ledge with a rappel anchor attached to a large tree. 5.7, 160 feet.

From here you can (1) rappel from the tree to the ground with double ropes down the *Chieu Hoi* dihedral; (2) rappel with one rope down *Granite Jungle* to a large ledge 70 feet below and do a second one-rope rappel from threaded blocks to the ground; or (3) continue up the crux pitch of *Chieu Hoi.* **Pitch Two:** Ascend the elegant, challenging dihedral (5.9-) up a thin crack. RPs and wired stoppers provide good protection in old pin scars. About 40 feet up is an obvious hand tra-

Kate McEwen enjoys the beautiful granite along Dislocation Direct.

verse left along a crack. Protection is good on this challenging 5.9 crux. The traverse ends at a sloping ramp and a belay at a small tree. 50 feet, 5.9. From the end of the climb traverse the ramp left to the *Coke Bottle* rappel route.

Thumb Butte

Rising like a sentinel above downtown Prescott, Thumb Butte is the city's primary landmark. Its proximity to town and the fast approach (30 minutes), coupled with the high quality of climbs, make this a popular destination for locals. Due to Thumb Butte's volcanic origins, the 1–2 pitch traditional climbs here are quite different in character from nearby Granite Mountain. Thumb Butte is composed of 14-million-year-old latite, which has a much different texture than other volcanic rocks such as basalt or welded tuff. From a distance the lumpy, broken-looking rock doesn't look all that enticing for climbing, but once most people touch fingers to stone they become converts. Most of the climbs here offer short crack segments linked together by beautiful faces studded with numerous solid and positive holds that are a joy to ascend.

Thumb Butte isn't large, but its geography is surprisingly complex. Numerous gullies carve the rock into separate buttresses, each with its own approach challenges and separate descents. Most of the descents entail some third-class scrambling with noticeable exposure; use care on your descents and don't hesitate to use a rope.

Most of the climbing on the Butte faces south or west. This aspect, combined with the dark rock that holds heat well, makes this a good climbing spot for much of the winter. Peregrine falcons nest on the face, and the Forest Service has imposed a climbing ban that usually lasts from February through July to protect them.

McNeill Mann on The Rigging

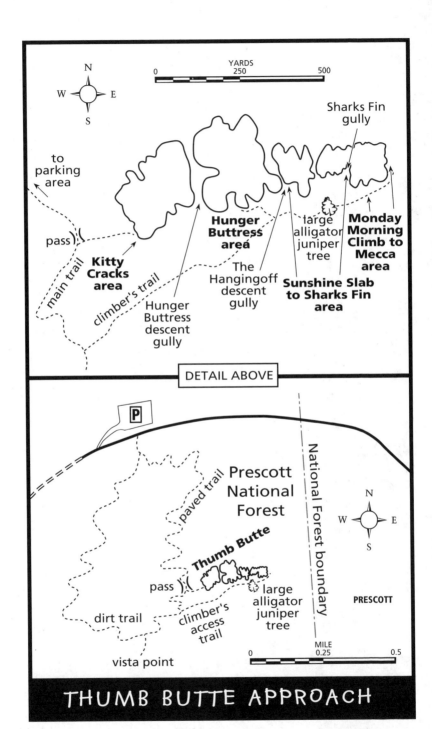

THUMB BUTTE APPROACH

THUMB BUTTE OVERVIEW

Kitty Cracks area

Sharks Fin gully descent

Hotdog in a Bun

approach

Sunshine Slab

Mecca

THUMB BUTTE BETA

Drive time from Tucson ▲ 3½ hours
Drive time from Phoenix ▲ 1½ hours
Drive time from Flagstaff ▲ 1½ hours

Getting there: Prescott lies 95 miles northwest of Phoenix and 95 miles southwest of Flagstaff. From the south, drive north on I-17 to SR 69 (exit 262). This highway leads directly to Prescott. From the north, drive south on I-17 to exit 278, marked Highway 169 and Cherry Road. Follow SR 169 southwest to the junction with SR 69 and turn right.

From either direction, once you are on SR 69, follow it north and west to Prescott. (See the Granite Mountain and Thumb Butte map in the previous section.) In town is a prominent junction with SR 89. Stay in the left lane at this junction and follow signs to Gurley Street. Follow Gurley to Courthouse Square, the center of historic downtown Prescott. Continue west on Gurley Street. About a mile west of downtown, Gurley takes a big left bend and becomes Thumb Butte Road. This road passes directly under the north flank of Thumb Butte several miles west of Courthouse Square, where a paved parking lot is located on the right. Park here for the approach to all of the climbs. Thumb Butte Road turns to dirt immediately beyond this parking lot.

Approach: 30 minutes. The simplest and most pleasant approach to all the climbs is up the paved trail on the north side of the butte. From the parking lot, walk south, across Thumb Butte Road, to the clearly marked, paved trail that leads steeply up the butte's lower flanks. Take the left trail fork 20 yards after you cross Thumb Butte Road. It takes about 20 minutes to hike up this steep trail to the ridge crest west of the butte, where the pavement ends and the West Side climbs are located. South Side climbs are accessed by 10 minutes of additional walking beyond this ridge, as described in the text.

Season and Elevation: Thumb Butte lies at 6000 feet, providing comfortable climbing throughout the year, though summers get pretty hot. See the following paragraph for seasonal closures.

Regulations: Closed for peregrine falcon nesting each year from approximately February through July. See the Granite Mountain section for more information. Thumb Butte is a Forest Service fee demo area. The current fee is $2 per vehicle (free on Wednesdays). Golden Eagle and Golden Access passes are accepted. The Forest Service does not maintain climber's trails. Please stick to already established trails to prevent a proliferation of new ones.

Camping: Primitive, no-fee camping is permitted at designated spots a few miles to the west on Thumb Butte Road on Prescott National Forest land (14-day maximum stay). Camping at Granite Basin is also an option—see the Granite Mountain chapter for details. Plenty of hotels are also available in Prescott.

Food and Supplies: Thumb Butte is very close to the city of Prescott. All services are easily available in town, including grocery stores, many restaurants, and a gear shop.

Gear: A standard rack will serve you well on most Thumb Butte climbs. Wired stoppers work especially well in the thin cracks that abound here. Some of the face climbs only protect well if you come equipped with a selection of micronuts (RPs). Wide cracks are common here; the individual climb descriptions note where large cams are particularly useful. Thumb Butte cracks are oddly lumpy, making nut placements in some cracks less than satisfying. Don't pass up good nut placements.

Emergency Services: A full-service hospital, Yavapai Regional Medical Center, is located at the corner of Iron Springs Road and Miller Valley Road: 1003 Willow Creek Rd., Prescott, AZ 86301. (928-445-2700) Additionally, the sheriff's office maintains a backcountry search and rescue team. (928-771-3260)

> **Kids and Dogs:** Dogs are allowed on a leash. Kids may enjoy the hike up and around the Thumb Butte trail, but the actual approach to the climbs is a bit much for little legs.

West Side Climbs—Kitty Cracks Area

To reach the climbs in the Kitty Cracks area, walk up the paved trail almost to its end. At the crest of the ridge west of the butte, about 20 yards before the pavement ends, is an interpretive sign titled Prehistoric Prescott Culture. The pavement veers right here and a wide, dirt path leads straight ahead. Follow this path for 2 minutes to the obvious buttress immediately right of a wide gully. All four West Side climbs are located on this buttress.

The descent for all four of these climbs is a scramble down the obvious gully, also known as the *Tourist Route* to the summit, immediately to the north (climber's left) of Kitty Cracks. For those seeking an extra challenge, the face right of *Little Chimney Right* offers a stout 5.10 top rope called *Puppy Face* that can be rigged with gear from just right of the top of *Little Chimney Right*.

1. KITTY CRACKS 5.7 ★★
FA: Rusty Baille 1990
This short, enjoyable route begins at a left-angling crack 5 feet left of *Big and Loose*. Work your way up the crack and the face above to a sloping ledge. Follow another left-leaning crack up from here to a second ledge. Step left here and ascend a blunt arête to the top. This climb offers good protection with small stoppers, but some of the placements are tricky. 100 feet. Alternatively, go straight up the face above the right side of the ledge, but this option is harder and poorly protected.

2. BIG AND LOOSE 5.6 ★★
This climb ascends the most prominent vertical crack on the left side of the buttress up to the obvious left-facing flake. Continue up the flake to its top and then up the low-angle face above. Don't let the name fool you—the rock isn't loose, and although the crack behind the flake is big, small cracks nearby offer good holds and protection. 100 feet.

3. LITTLE CHIMNEY LEFT 5.7 ★

This route takes the left side of the prominent, deep chimney 30 feet right of *Big and Loose*. Easy climbing leads to a couple of awkward crux moves at a bulge and then easier climbing to the top of the chimney. Easy face climbing on the slab above the left side of the chimney completes the climb on the same ledge where *Kitty Cracks* ends. 100 feet.

4. LITTLE CHIMNEY RIGHT 5.6 ★

This route goes up the right side of the same chimney as *Little Chimney Left*. The crux is turning the chockstone at the top of the chimney. From the top of the chockstone, you can move left to finish up the same face as *Little Chimney Left*, or head up a brushy gully to the top. 100 feet.

South Side Climbs

Most of the routes at Thumb Butte lie on the south side. To approach these climbs, follow the paved trail over the pass to where it turns to dirt (15–20 minutes). Continue along this dirt trail and begin counting turns at a sweeping left switchback with a park bench soon after the dirt begins. To your left at the second right-bending switchback (after about

200 yards on the dirt trail) stands a green metal fence post. A narrow dirt climber's path leads southeast past this post, down the slope beneath all of the South Side climbs. Thumb Butte's south side is broken into several buttresses separated by gullies or areas of broken rock. Refer to the description of each buttress for final approach information.

HUNGER BUTTRESS AREA

From the main South Side trail, approach these climbs via a faint path that cuts up an open, grassy slope below and right of *Hotdog in a Bun*. The descent for all of the climbs in this area cuts north, toward the center ridgeline of the butte, then descends a narrow corridor west to a gully that takes you back south to the base of the climbs.

1. TURKEY FRANKS 5.8 ★
FA: Mike Goff and partners 1980s

This route ascends the obvious chimney that cuts the buttress. Moderate climbing leads up to the prominent roof. Turn the roof on the right and continue up the crack. Veer left at a pine tree near the top. Protection can be tricky low down because of the flaring nature of many of the cracks, but the crux is well protected. Beware of loose rock at the

roof. Wired stoppers and medium to large cams (to #4) protect the route. This route is moderate for its grade. 100 feet.

2. CUT THE MUSTARD 5.8 ★★
FA: Mike Goff and partners 1980s
Begin at the same place as *Turkey Franks* but traverse a horizontal crack onto the right-hand face. Ascend the nice crack that splits the face. There are abundant small holds on this surprisingly steep face. Protection at the crux is good, but it is somewhat strenuous to place. Twenty feet up the angle eases and the holds get larger, making the climbing 5.3, but protection is difficult. Step left at the top of the low-angle slab to join *Turkey Franks* above its roof. The difficulty increases here to 5.5, but protection is again good. Wired stoppers, RPs, and small to medium cams protect the pitch. 100 feet.

3. PICKLE RELISH 5.9 R or 5.9 TR ★★
FA: David Lovejoy, Carol Petrelli, Steve Munsell 1980s
This is the beautiful face to the left of the *Hotdog in a Bun* chimney. Protection is sparse and can be tricky to place, so take advantage of good pro when you find it. A good alternative is to top-rope this climb from natural gear that is easily placed at the top of *Hotdog in a Bun*. 120 feet.

4. HOTDOG IN A BUN 5.7 ★★★
FA: David Lovejoy, Dwight Bradley 1969
This is a fun climb with a little bit of everything. Scramble up to the base of the prominent chimney on the buttress immediately right of the one containing *Turkey Franks*. Follow the chimney the whole way up, enjoying the many face moves along the way. 130 feet.

SUNSHINE SLAB TO SHARKS FIN AREA

To reach this area, continue east on the main trail beneath the south face of the Butte until you reach a prominent alligator juniper tree with a flat dirt area beneath it and flat boulders immediately to the west of it. This is a good staging area for the climbs in this section. To reach the base of climbs 6–9, move up and left from the alligator juniper. All other climbs are accessed by moving right from the tree. Unless otherwise noted, the

Opposite: The climbing on Sunshine Slab *is as fun as it gets.*

descent for all of these routes is via the *Sharks Fin* gully, which entails third- to fourth-class scrambling.

5. LEFT OF SICKLE 5.4 ★★

This is a delightful route that provides quintessential Thumb Butte climbing at a moderate grade. The route ascends the brown, varnished face left of the prominent, sickle-shaped crack that is a landmark for this section of the butte. Begin just left of a large talus block lodged in the ground at the base of the rock. Ascend the face, wandering left or right to find slightly harder or easier climbing. Protection is sparse low down but becomes more abundant higher up. Wired stoppers on long runners are very useful on this long, 150-foot pitch. The most expedient descent is to scramble down the third- to fourth-class gully left of the climb (called *Hangingoff*). There are several exposed sections on this descent.

6. THE SICKLE 5.10a ★★★
FA: Mike Goff and partners 1970s

This gorgeous climb is on the stiff side of moderate, but it is definitely worth doing if you are up to the grade. It follows the obvious right-facing dihedral over a small roof to a thinner crack and very thin footwork

SUNSHINE SLAB TO SHARKS FIN AREA, LEFT

above before traversing right under the large roof to the belay. Don't forget to place protection for the second on this traversing line under the roof. 120 feet. The second pitch is shared with *One Hard Move* and continues up along a crack to a lower-angle gully to the top. Better yet, finish on the second pitch of *Sunshine Slab*. This is the variation shown on the route photo. From the top it is easiest to use the *Hangingoff* descent described for *Left of Sickle*.

7. ONE HARD MOVE 5.7 ★
FA: David Lovejoy and partners 1970s

Although this climb is short, its crux definitely provides an interesting move. Begin in the low-angle, left-facing dihedral crack just right of the prominent sickle-shaped crack. Ascend this crack and the face to its left on moves that are more enjoyable than they appear to be from below. At the obvious weakness go right, up the right wall of the dihedral. Steep climbing here provides the crux. This pitch finishes on *Sunshine Slab*'s intermediate belay ledge, which has a large eyebolt. 100 feet. Finish up the crack to the gully above or, preferably, climb the second pitch of *Sunshine Slab*, as shown on the route photograph. Wired stoppers and small to medium cams protect this climb well. Descend as for *Sunshine Slab*.

8. SUNSHINE SLAB 5.6 ★★★
FA: Communal

A Thumb Butte classic! Ascend the beautiful slab that lies to the right of the prominent *Sickle* roof. Third-class scrambling leads to a small ledge at the base of the face. The route can be done in one long pitch (160 feet), or you can set up an intermediate belay on a comfortable ledge with a huge eyebolt

The steep upper section of Sunshine Slab *offers climbers a dizzying choice of positive holds.*

SUNSHINE SLAB TO SHARKS FIN AREA. RIGHT

Sharks Fin gully descent

alligator juniper

approach

Hanging off descent

on the left side of the slab about two-thirds of the way up. **Pitch One:** Work up the left side of the slab, turning a roof on the left, and run up to the belay ledge. Don't pass up any good placements on this pitch, as protection can be difficult to place. **Pitch Two:** From this ledge move back right onto the center of the slab and pick your favorite line up a steep face that is studded with exceptional holds and riddled with good cracks for protection. From the top it is equally easy to move left to the

Hangingoff descent gully (described for *Left of Sickle*) or scramble right (very exposed) to the top of the *Sharks Fin* gully.

9. TWIN CRACKS LEFT 5.7 ★★
FA: Mike Goff and others 1970s

Approach this climb by ascending the lower portion of *Sharks Fin* gully and cutting left to the base of the buttress that sports two cracks. This chimney looks claustrophobic from below, but it yields enjoyable climbing that employs a variety of techniques, including fun face climbing and stemming. Large cams are useful. 70 feet. Descend the *Sharks Fin* gully to the right of the climb.

10. TWIN CRACKS RIGHT 5.8 ★★
FA: Mike Goff and others 1970s

This crack is appropriately named, as it is nearly a carbon copy of its left twin, though this one may be a bit more strenuous. 70 feet. Its descent is also the same.

Alison Kopinto grapples with the slot on Twin Cracks Left.

11. YELLOW EDGE 5.8 ★★★

FA: David Lovejoy, Mike Goff 1980s

Short but very sweet! This airy gem ascends the arête of the upper-most buttress on the right side of the *Sharks Fin* gully. Wired stoppers and small to medium cams provide good protection, although it is strenuous to place. 40 feet. Descend the *Sharks Fin* gully.

12. THE RIGGING 5.7 ★

FA: Steve Munsell and others 1970s

This climb begins in the boxy slot 10 feet right of *Yellow Edge*. Ascend the slot and move left at its top around a small overhang. Cut back right beneath a second overhang and finish up that roof's right side. 50 feet. Descend the *Sharks Fin* gully.

Phil Latham reaches for the top on The Rigging.

Sharks
Fin
gully
↓

YELLOW EDGE TO
HIDDEN CHIMNEY

⑪

⑫   ⑬

13. HIDDEN CHIMNEY 5.6 ★

About two-thirds of the way up the *Sharks Fin* gully lies a deep chimney on the right. A petroglyph chiseled by some Prescott pioneers says "sines" on the buttress right of this chimney. *Hidden Chimney* isn't really a chimney, but rather takes the attractive crack that splits the face on the chimney's left wall. It ends on the ridge crest just 40 feet right of the top of the *Sharks Fin* gully. 50 feet. Descend the *Sharks Fin* gully.

14. SHARKS FIN 5.7 ★★

FA: Mike Goff and partners 1970s

This climb tackles the prominent buttress immediately right of *Sharks Fin* gully on airy face moves. It begins in a wide crack that runs between two roofs (crux) and then moves out onto the face above. Bring large cams for the start and long slings for tying off chockstones and threadthroughs. Move left at the top to reach *Sharks Fin* gully. 150 feet.

MONDAY MORNING CLIMB TO MECCA AREA

To reach this area, walk right from the alligator juniper, past the *Sharks Fin* gully. *Heart Route* and *Mecca* lie around the corner to the left, on a southeast-facing buttress.

15. MONDAY MORNING CLIMB 5.8 ★★★

FA: David Lovejoy, Mike Goff 1970s

This exquisite climb tackles the center of the buttress right of *Sharks Fin*. **Pitch One:** The climb begins in a squeeze slot near the left edge of the buttress, then steps right along a right-angling crack through a bulge.

One strenuous, tricky, but well-protected move gets you over the bulge and onto the delicate face above. Tiptoe up this beautiful face on small, positive edges to a belay at a large ledge. Medium cams protect the initial crack. For those who love the art of nutcraft, RPs and wired stoppers fit in some wonderfully creative placements that provide adequate protection on the easier face moves above. 110 feet. **Pitch Two:** A short, easy pitch up the buttress behind the belay ledge finishes the climb on the summit ridge. Move left to the *Sharks Fin* gully descent. Watch for wasps and possibly rattlesnakes in the lower cracks!

MONDAY MORNING CLIMB TO MECCA AREA, RIGHT

to Sharks Fin gully

approach

16. RACK AND PINYON 5.6 ★

FA: David Lovejoy, Amparo Rifa 1980s

This route provides enjoyable, clean climbing. **Pitch One:** Begin as for *Heart Route*, but veer left once you clear the roof low down. Face climbing leads to a belay at a prominent horizontal crack. 70 feet. **Pitch Two:** This pitch entails more face climbing above the belay and finishes on an arête that forms the left edge of a clean, narrow face. 120 feet. To descend, continue up the ridge to the *Sharks Fin* gully.

17. HEART ROUTE 5.6 ★★

FA: Bob Miller, Chuck Carpenter 1969

Pitch One: Ascend a short, mellow chimney, then trend slightly right to a comfortable belay stance below a prominent dihedral. 70 feet.

Granite Mountain rises a short distance behind and right of Thumb Butte. Together, they provide Prescott area climbers a wealth of quality, diverse routes close to town.

Pitch Two: Ascend an enjoyable crack in an open book past an optional belay at the top of the crack. From here, step slightly right to continue up another enjoyable crack to the summit. Medium to large pro is useful. 120 feet. Descend the *Sharks Fin* gully.

18. MECCA 5.9 ★★★
FA: Rusty Baille, Royal Robbins 1971

This is the classic crack splitting a dome-shaped face that you can see as you approach Thumb Butte from Prescott. It's as good as it looks, definitely one of the best routes on the Butte! It is most easily approached by walking down east (right) from the alligator juniper around the nose of the dome-shaped buttress on the Butte's east flank. Scramble up a gully and traverse left to the base of the prominent crack. The route ascends the wide crack through a band of discontinuous roofs, then runs up the obvious crack above. Step left at the top and finish in a flaring chimney. Small to large protection will all be useful. 120 feet. Use the *Sharks Fin* gully to descend.

Sedona

Sedona climbing is something special. Summiting one of the spires that rise amidst some of the most beautiful scenery in the United States is an experience that few climbers ever forget. Most Sedona routes are difficult and committing, but a few more moderate gems stand out for weekend climbers.

Sedona climbing takes place on two ancient sandstone formations, the Coconino Sandstone and the Schnebly Hill Formation, deposited 270–280 million years ago. The Coconino is a blonde sandstone that was deposited as desert sand dunes at a time when Sedona sat in a desert the size and dryness of the Sahara. The climb *Four Flying Apaches* tackles a spectacular buttress formed of this stone. Sedona's famous Red Rocks are composed of the Schnebly Hill Formation, which was deposited earlier than the Coconino during a time when Sedona formed an arid coastline of the great supercontinent Pangaea. Sand dunes marched right to the seashore, giving the area a look similar to today's Atacama Desert in South America. The Schnebly Hill Formation hosts the majority of Sedona's climbing routes, including most of the routes listed here. One distinctive feature of this formation that you will encounter on many Sedona climbs is a 5- to 10-foot thick gray band of sandy limestone sandwiched between the layers of red sandstone. The "limestone band," as

Jonathon Reckling steps out on the wild third pitch of Four Flying Apaches.

it is known by climbers, offers the most solid stone you will encounter on Sedona climbs and it hosts some memorable face traverses, such as those on *Mars Attacks!*, *Goliath*, and *Streaker Spire*.

All Sedona sandstone is very soft. Holds can pop off at any time and most routes cross some loose rock. The prevalence of long, difficult routes,

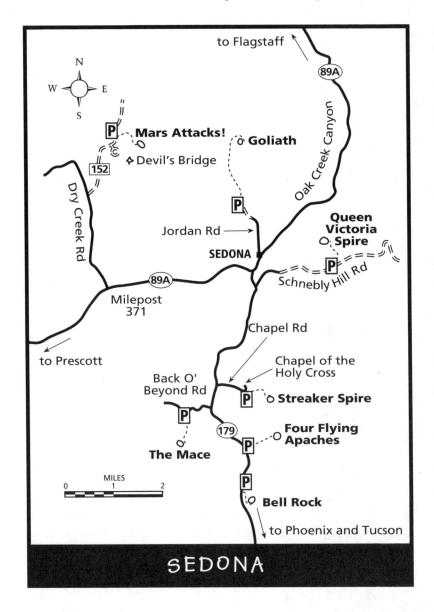

Nate Burk is engulfed in a sea of sandstone on the first pitch of Goliath.

the loose rock, and the sometimes suspect protection have combined to give Sedona climbing an aura of difficulty and danger. Tim Toula, one of the area's guidebook authors, nourished this aura in his entertaining guidebook *A Better Way to Die*. You needn't fear imminent death every time you venture onto a Sedona climb, but the climbing here is serious and should be treated with respect. Many Sedona climbs entail at least one "horror" pitch of one type or another. I've tried to include in this guide only climbs that lack such pitches and that provide good protection. What constitutes a horror pitch is, of course, in the eye of the beholder, but all of the climbs included here can be (and routinely are) ascended safely by careful, well-equipped, competent parties. Sedona is not the place to immediately push your leading limit. It is a very good idea to start with a route well beneath your usual leading ability. *Bell Rock* provides an excellent, one-pitch introduction to Sedona climbing that entails less commitment than most routes, and *Goliath* is another great first choice. Wearing a helmet is always a good idea, but it is especially important here.

It is hard to get up a Sedona spire without climbing an off-width crack, a skill that many climbers rarely employ. Expect to grunt and groan on sections of most of the routes listed here. You will be rewarded with magnificent views, a sense of accomplishment, and the satisfaction that comes from being in a place accessible only to those few who know how to use a rope and who are willing to work for their summits.

First-time climbers to Sedona usually either catch the bug and return frequently or they vow never to return. If you catch the bug, there are a few classic 5.9 routes that wouldn't fit in this guide to put on your list after you've done all the routes listed here. Consider doing *Dr. Rubo's Wild Ride* (5.9), *Dresdoom* (5.9+ R), *Screaming Besingi* (5.8/5.9) or *Oak Creek Spire* (5.9). Some of these routes take the seriousness level up a notch from the climbs included in this book, but by the time you've climbed the routes described here you will have an excellent idea of what Sedona climbing entails. All are listed in *A Better Way to Die* and the most recent Sedona guidebook, *Castles in the Sand*, by David Bloom.

SEDONA BETA

Drive time from Tucson ▲ 3½ hours
Drive time from Phoenix ▲ 1½ hours
Drive time from Flagstaff ▲ about 45 minutes

Getting there: To reach Sedona from the south, travel north on I-17 to exit 298. Proceed north on SR 179 15 miles to Sedona. From the north, either travel south on I-17 to exit 298 and continue as described above, or take SR 89A south from Flagstaff down into and through the very scenic Oak Creek Canyon to Sedona. Downtown Sedona is defined by the junction of highways 89A and 179. The driving directions to each climb are listed separately, beginning at this intersection.

Approach: All of the routes listed here ascend independent walls or spires. Driving and hiking directions are listed separately for each one. The approach hiking times range from 20 minutes to 1 hour.

Season and Elevation: The Sedona climbs lie between 4500–5500 feet, with moderate temperatures most of the year. Spring and fall are best. Summer temperatures routinely climb into the high 90s to low 100s, and monsoon rainstorms are a real threat from July through September on these long climbs. Winter climbing can be chilly, but temperatures are often comfortable for extended periods of time.

Regulations: All climbs listed here are on public land belonging to the Coconino National Forest. Parking at some of the trailheads is very limited, and all parking within the national forest requires you to purchase a Sedona Red Rocks Pass. Passes, which cost $5 a day in 2006, can be purchased from the ranger stations in the Village of Oak Creek and West Sedona, at Sedona area visitor centers, and at a few automatic vending machines at the most popular trailheads.

Camping: Several Forest Service campgrounds are located in the scenic Oak Creek Canyon. The nearest of these, Manzanita, is 6 miles up the canyon from Sedona at 4800 feet and is open year-round. It has drinking water. Bootlegger, the next campground north, is 9 miles from Sedona. It doesn't have drinking water and is open only from mid-April to mid-fall. Showers are available at Cave Spring Campground, 14 miles up the canyon at 5500 feet. It is open seasonally.

Food and Supplies: The climbs ring the small tourist city of Sedona. Grocery stores and many restaurants are available within 5 miles of all climbs.

Gear: A standard Sedona rack consists of wired stoppers and a double set of Friends or Camalots, plus large cams for off-widths. Carrying one or two #4 Camalots or their equivalent is commonplace here, and large hexes and tube chocks or Big Bros can be of use. Bring some extra shoulder-length slings. See the description of each climb for route-specific gear suggestions. The nearest gear stores are in Flagstaff, a 45-minute drive away.

Emergency Services: Verde Valley Medical Center is located at 3700 West Highway 89A, 3.6 miles west of the downtown Sedona road junction. (928-204-4116)

Kids and Dogs: These are long, committing climbs—better to leave the family (including canines) to take a gorgeous hike or mountain-bike ride in the surrounding area rather than have them hang out at the base.

Goliath

Approach: From the SR 89A /179 junction in downtown Sedona, travel 0.3 mile east on 89A and turn left (north) on Jordan Road. This is the street immediately past the first stoplight (at Forest Road) after the highway junction. Drive 0.7 mile on Jordan Road to its terminus at Park Ridge Road. Turn left on Park Ridge Road, which turns to dirt after 0.2 mile. Continue up this dirt road for an additional 0.5 mile to a parking area at its end (1.4 total miles from SR 89A).

The approach hike takes about 1 hour. The Brins Mesa trail heads north from the trailhead, but rather than taking this trail, veer right (northeast) from the trailhead into the large open field that lies to the right. This is the abandoned shooting range. Cross the field and drop down into the wash (Mormon Canyon) at its far side. Walk north up the pleasant wash for about 40 minutes. There are few distinctive landmarks, and the crux of the approach is finding the right place to exit the wash. A small tributary wash enters from the left (as you look upstream) after about 15 minutes, and another tributary comes in from the right after 25 minutes. At each junction stay in the obvious main wash. *Goliath*, *The Mushroom*, and a large, unnamed tower all come into view to your

right (northeast) after about 30 minutes. *The Mushroom* (whose top is visible from the trailhead) is the 600-foot-tall blonde spire, and *Goliath* is the smaller red spire to its left. The unnamed tower, which is blocky and mostly red, is the most distinctive of the three from this vantage point. Soon thereafter you reach a small section of slickrock in the wash, the first you've encountered. The right bank of the wash here consists of a 10-foot-high red sandstone wall. This is the first of several short slickrock sections.

After about 40 minutes you reach a longer section of slickrock with an 8-foot-high red sandstone wall, this time on the left (west). This is the place to exit the wash to the east. A cairn is occasionally found at this junction. The unnamed tower is prominent from here, now standing to your southeast. *Goliath* and *The Mushroom* are due east, visible in glimpses through the trees. Turn right (northeast) up a small, brushy tributary gully. Follow it for 20 yards and turn right again (east) on a small boulder field. These boulders are outwash from another gully, which you reach after another 30 yards of walking. Continue up this gully for about 100 yards to a large red boulder, where you move left into another, very small, brushy gully that heads directly toward *Goliath*'s west face. After 70 yards in this gully you scramble up a slickrock ledge that deposits you in an open area with your first unobstructed view of *Goliath* straight ahead. You soon reach the head of the gully at a resistant rock band. Turn left and follow this band for about 50 yards until you can scramble over it. From here head straight up the open slopes beneath *Goliath*'s north face to the obvious saddle east of the tower. It will take you 15–20 minutes to reach the saddle after you exit the wash.

GOLIATH 5.6 or 5.9 ★★★

FA: Scott Baxter, G. Douglass 1970s

With the exception of one optional 5.9 boulder problem to surmount the final summit block, this is one of the most moderate spire climbs in the Sedona area. It provides enjoyable climbing, incredible exposure, and little loose rock by Sedona standards. *Goliath* is more secluded than most Sedona spires, and the scenery is stunning. You can easily forego the final 5.9 move, making *Goliath* the premier moderate spire climb in the area. Adding the final move provides a bit of extra spice and deposits you on a classic summit.

The route begins on the east face and finishes on the south and west faces, providing a grand tour of the spire. Most parties can complete the climb in about 2 hours. Even a light, standard rack protects the climb well, but the climb does have a wide crack, so a few large cams (to #4 Camalot) are helpful. Pitches one and two wander, requiring long slings to avoid rope drag. You will need 2 ropes for the rappel.

Pitch One: The climb starts in the obvious wide crack that rises directly above the saddle. Follow the crack for about 40 feet, until a series of ledges offers an easy traverse left across the face. You are aiming for a chimney 25 feet to the left. When you reach the chimney climb it for a

GOLIATH
LOWER ROUTE

30 feet

slung block
anchor

40 feet

150 feet

pitch 2
goes around
the corner

PP
1

P

few feet, passing a fixed pin, and step left onto a large ledge atop a light colored band of rock 5 feet below the obvious gray limestone band. Belay at 2 fixed pins on the ledge. Beware of rope drag on the traverse. Protection on the traverse is skimpy, but the climbing is moderate. 5.5, 80 feet. **Pitch Two:** Climb any one of the several weaknesses in the limestone band above the belay, then traverse the band left around the corner, onto the spire's south face. The climbing is easy, but the exposure is huge and there is an exciting step-across move as you round the corner. Plenty of protection is available in the limestone band at your feet. Remember to protect the second on this traverse. Continue the leftward traverse to a small tree at the base of a chimney. 5.4, 80 feet. **Pitch Three:** Climb this chimney, which has cracks on both walls that accept good protection, to a large ledge 40 feet up. Another chimney heads up and right from here. Climb that chimney to a belay at its top. 5.6, 80 feet. **Pitch Four:**

30 feet

slung block anchor

40 feet

GOLIATH
UPPER ROUTE

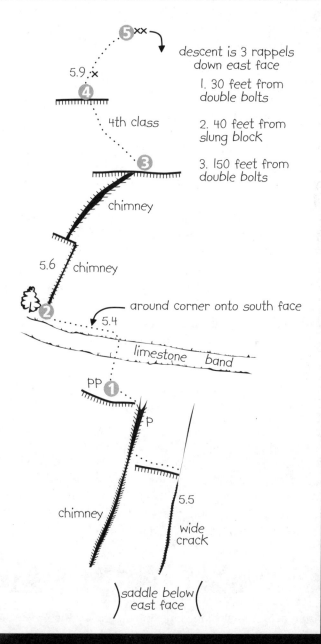

5 xx

descent is 3 rappels
down east face

1. 30 feet from
double bolts

5.9 :x

4

2. 40 feet from
slung block

4th class

3. 150 feet from
double bolts

3

chimney

5.6 chimney

2 around corner onto south face

5.4

limestone band

PP 1

P

chimney

5.5

wide
crack

saddle below
east face

GOLIATH

Here you have two choices, both fourth class. The main route heads 60 feet up and left to a glorious ledge on the west face of the spire directly below the final summit block. A bolt is situated on this headwall. Even if you don't plan to do the 5.9 boulder move onto the summit, this ledge makes a worthy destination, as the views are panoramic. Belay from gear on this ledge. Alternatively, if you are in a hurry and don't plan to do the 5.9 summit move, you can head up and right for about 30 feet, over a series of blocks, to a ledge that lies southeast and directly below the final headwall. You will find slings around a boulder here that form the rappel anchor for the descent down the east face. **Pitch Five:** Once again, you have a choice here. To reach the true summit clip the bolt on the headwall and do a steep and awkward move onto the summit block. There is real ankle-busting potential on this move, so be careful! From there it is a 20-foot climb to the top. A double-bolt anchor lies on the east side of the summit. 5.9, 25 feet.

If you don't want to try your hand at this final move, you can scramble (fourth class) horizontally east from the ledge, directly under the overhanging summit block for 30 feet to the slung boulder rappel station mentioned in the pitch four description.

Descent: If you are on the summit block, make a 30-foot rappel east–southeast from the double-bolt top anchor to the slung boulder mentioned in pitch four. There are no chains on the top anchor, so bring a sling and rappel rings. If you didn't climb to the top, you will find yourself starting the descent at the slung boulder. It is a good idea to bring a long sling (about 15 feet) to augment or replace the slings already in place. Rappel 40 feet southeast from the boulder to a large ledge, aiming for the double bolts with chains that are visible at the top of the long crack/chimney system that you climbed to begin pitch one. Make a final 150-foot rappel (2 ropes) east from these bolts with chains down the crack system to the saddle at the base of the climb. Beware of dislodging loose rocks in this chimney.

Queen Victoria

Approach: From the junction between Arizona Highways 89A and 179 in downtown Sedona, travel south 0.4 mile on SR 179 to the clearly marked intersection with Schnebly Hill Road. Turn left (east) on Schnebly Hill Road and drive 1.8 miles to a small pullout on the left. If this pullout is

full, any of several other pullouts nearby work equally well. Schnebly Hill Road is paved for the first half mile and is a good gravel road from there to the parking area.

From the parking area, *Queen Victoria* is visible on the ridge across the wash to the north. It is the small, sleek spire immediately right of the larger, more rounded Pointed Dome. To the right of *Queen Victoria* is a broad saddle and then the even more massive Moose's Butte. The approach takes about 30–45 minutes. From the parking area, drop down the short slope to the wash. Turn right and follow the wide trail along the far side of the wash for about 300 yards until you encounter a small gully leading up the steep slope on the left (north). Ascend this gully in the direction of *Queen Victoria*. There really isn't much of a trail in this lower portion of the approach. You can head up the slope anywhere, but the gully offers the easiest passage.

After you gain about 100 feet of elevation, the slope moderates and you find yourself on a much flatter bench directly below Moose's Butte. The saddle between it and *Queen Victoria* is visible about 400 vertical feet above you. A better trail exists here, though many climbers never find it. Contour the right flank of the deep valley to your left, which leads to the saddle between Moose's Butte and *Queen Victoria*. Skirt a short cliff below Moose's Butte on the left, ending up in the major gully that leads to the saddle. Follow this gully to the saddle. The route's first pitch lies in the prominent chimney on the spire's east face and is clearly visible from the saddle. A short walk up the ridge brings you to a small ramp that leads 20 feet left (south) to the base of the first pitch, a chimney.

QUEEN VICTORIA 5.7 ★★
FA: Chuck Martens

Queen Victoria is one of the most popular spires in Sedona. The route is aesthetic and ends on an airy but comfortable summit with spectacular

QUEEN VICTORIA

views of Sedona and Oak Creek Canyon. There is a lot of loose rock on parts of the route, especially on the large belay ledges and on the low-angle ramps that connect the more difficult climbing. But the route offers plenty of good protection and can be climbed safely. The route lies on the east and southeast faces, offering cool climbing in the afternoon. Most parties take 2–4 hours to complete the climb.

Bring a standard Sedona rack. The crux on pitch two is protected with a #4 Camalot, and a short section of easier climbing above the crux can be protected by a #5 Camalot if you want to lug it up the climb. A double set of Camalots from #½–#2 is useful, and small to medium wired stoppers work great in many of the cracks. Bring an ample supply of shoulder-length slings, as pitches two and three wander. Two ropes are needed for the descent.

Pitch One: Ascend the wide chimney, which has some nice cracks in the back of it for holds and protection, for 90 feet to a comfortable belay ledge with a double-bolt anchor. 5.6, 90 feet. **Pitch Two:** Step left off the belay ledge to a leftward-rising ramp that ends at a 10-foot-high, right-facing dihedral with a 4- to 5-inch crack in the back of it. This dihedral cuts the light-colored limestone band that girdles the tower. Ascend the off-width in the back of the dihedral (5.7) to a rubble-covered, leftward-rising ramp. A #4 Camalot protects the crux. Ascend the ramp to a belay at the base of a prominent dihedral/slot that has a beautiful crack in the back of it. Take care arranging this belay, as the rock is loose. A #1 and #2 Camalot help for the belay. 5.7, 90 feet. **Pitch Three:** Ascend the dihedral/slot. It starts with moderate chimney moves to the base of the beautiful crack. The crack provides elegant 5.7 climbing with perfect protection. Easy ramps lead up and right from the top of the crack to the summit. 5.7, 80 feet. **Descent:** Do a double-rope rappel east from an obvious double-bolt anchor right on the summit. This rap puts you at a second double-bolt anchor located on a ledge at the top of the limestone band. This second rap anchor is visible from the summit. A double-rope rappel east from these bolts lands you at the base of the climb. Both rap anchors are equipped with chains.

Streaker Spire

Approach: A chain of towers occupies a north–south-trending ridge be-hind (east of) the famous Chapel of the Holy Cross. *Streaker Spire* is the southernmost of these summits. The approach begins from a parking area immediately below the chapel. From the junction of Highways 179 and 89A, drive 2.9 miles south on SR 179. Turn left here (at milepost 310.8) onto Chapel Road. This road ends at the chapel after 0.8 mile. A number of small parking lots are available around the chapel, one of the busiest tourist sites in all of Sedona. Please avoid the lots marked "Church parking only." You can also park along the road just outside of the church gate.

The climb begins from the notch to the north of Streaker Spire, between it and the taller Christianity Tower. The trail starts at the largest parking lot on the right side of the road just below the steep switchback up to the church. Take the time to find the climber's trail, as it is obvious and makes for speedy walking once you are on it. The trail stays low at first and then becomes fainter, but it is marked by cairns as it contours up and right below the group's northern spires. Scramble up a few slabs below Christianity Tower, the spire immediately north of Streaker, and then finish up the gully below the notch between Christianity and Streaker. The approach takes 30–40 minutes.

STREAKER SPIRE 5.7+ ★★
FA: Scott Baxter, Karl Karlstrom, R. Hardwick, G. Parker 1972
Streaker Spire is a handsome and popular tower. It offers interesting,

2 raps down north face using 1 rope

STREAKER SPIRE

well-protected climbing on soft but generally good rock. The crux dihedral on pitch three makes the climb, offering beautiful and intriguing moves up an overhanging dihedral. Because the route ascends the north and west faces of the rock, it provides cool morning climbing on hot days. Most parties complete the route in 2–4 hours.

Bring a standard Sedona rack, with Camalots through #3. Long slings are useful on this traversing route. The rappels consume every inch of a 50-meter rope, so use extreme caution and bring a longer rope if you have one.

Pitch One: From the notch, scramble up a short face to gain the ledge formed by the top of the hard, gray limestone band. Traverse rightward (west) along this ledge and around the corner to a small belay stance at the base of a left-angling crack system. 5.2, 120 feet. **Pitch Two:** Ascend the widening crack, and as it peters out, step right into an easy chimney. Belay on a large ledge at the top of the chimney. 5.7, 100 feet. **Pitch Three:** This stimulating crux pitch reaches the summit by ascending the overhanging dihedral above the belay. This pitch rewards climbers who are creative in their move selection. 5.7+, 100 feet. **Descent:** Two single-rope rappels descend the north face. The first set of anchors is at the summit, and the second set lies left (east) of the belay at the top of pitch two. The last rappel ends at the notch where you began the climb.

Both rappels consume a whole 50-meter rope, so bring a longer rope if you have one.

The Mace

Approach: From the SR 89A/179 junction in downtown Sedona travel 3.3 miles south on SR 179 to Back O' Beyond Road, where you turn right (west). On the left, 0.65 mile down this road is the parking area for the Cathedral Rocks trailhead. Park here and follow the trail southwest for about a mile up to the rocks. *The Mace* is the obvious hammerhead spire at the left side of the group. Hike up slickrock from the trail to the base of the northeast face (facing the parking area) to begin the climb. The hike takes about 20 minutes.

Charlie Crocker poised to jump the chasm on the descent of The Mace. *(Photo: Charity Khan)*

THE MACE 5.9+ ★★★
FA: Bob Kamps, T. M. Herbert, Dave Rearick 1957

The Mace was the first Sedona spire ever climbed, and it is still the most famous climb here. It is generally well protected and ascends some of the more solid stone in the area. Few climbers avoid having butterflies in their stomachs as they lean across the void on the last pitch, and the heart-stopping jump down from the summit to the top of the adjacent spire is the stuff of legends, as well as many broken ankles! The author joined the long list of casualties from this jump after his first ascent of the tower in 1989. At that time it was almost unthinkable to ascend the tower without making the famous leap, and the rather dubious top anchors made it seem plausible that the leap was less risky than a rappel. Fortunately, long ago a solid top anchor was installed that makes the leap entirely optional. Many climbers still take the plunge, but now I prefer to get my thrills on the exciting route and take the pedestrian way down!

Pitch One: Begin on an easy, right-angling ramp that lies on the right side of the face. Follow the ramp as it becomes a chimney capped by a small overhang formed at the base of the resistant limestone band.

Charity Kahn tiptoes across the airy third pitch traverse on The Mace.
(Photo: Charlie Crocker)

THE MACE

2 raps down back, 2 ropes

I rope

5.7 moves take you over the roof to a belay with double bolts on top of the limestone band. 5.7, 100 feet. **Pitch Two:** Climb the crack above the belay, with a 5.9- crux low down. The crack gets progressively wider above, until it turns into a tight squeeze chimney. An optional #5 Camalot protects the 5-inch section of crack near the top. Step left at the top onto a comfortable belay ledge with bolts. 5.9-, 100 feet. *Note:* If you need to bail off the route here, you can make your way up from the belay at the top of this pitch to the notch where one double-rope rappel will get you to the ground. **Pitch Three:** Step left off the belay ledge onto an airy, bolt-protected traverse that ends at a wide crack. Ascend this crack and squeeze chimney to a belay on a ledge with an eyebolt, where the chimney becomes very wide. 5.8, 90 feet. **Pitch Four:** Slide deep into the bowels of this beautiful chimney and ascend an off-width crack that lies within it. The crux of the route lies near the top of this crack where it widens to 4 inches. A bolt protects the crux, but #3 and #4 Camalots provide additional protection. Belay from bolts on the summit of *The Mace*'s subsidiary tower. 5.9+, 80 feet. **Pitch Five:** Screw up enough courage to lean across the void that separates this subsidiary tower from the main summit. With your hands on one tower and your feet on the other, shuffle right a couple of steps to a bolt. Mantle up onto the wall above

The author prepares to enter the bowels of the crux chimney on The Mace. *(Photo: Charlie Crocker)*

and finish with easy climbing to the spacious summit of *The Mace*. 5.8, 40 feet. **Descent:** From the true summit, either do a short rappel to the top of the subsidiary summit or scramble down the tower as far as you can and make the exciting leap across the gap between the towers. Either way you end up at a bolted rappel anchor on the subsidiary summit. From here rappel the back side of the tower down the gap between the two towers using 2 ropes (120 feet) to the notch between the main and subsidiary tower, at almost the same height as the top of pitch two. From here make a short scramble to another bolt anchor and rappel 100 feet to a saddle between *The Mace* and the adjacent tower. Scramble back to the base of the route from the saddle.

The route protects well if you bring a generous rack that includes several large cams, as noted in the descriptions for each pitch.

Four Flying Apaches

Approach: This wall sits high above most other rocks, so the approach is a hoof. The fact that the route is new and has yet to develop a defined climb-er's trail doesn't help matters. There are many possible ways to approach the climb, but the following way is direct and relatively straightforward. From the SR 89A/179 T-junction in downtown Sedona travel south on SR 179 for

FOUR FLYING
APACHES APPROACH

approach

4.5 miles to a large gravel pullout on the left (east) at milepost 308.9. The climb ascends the left skyline of the tall, blonde cliff of Coconino Sandstone that dominates the eastern horizon from the parking area. Its summit is marked point 5729 on topographic maps. This is a popular trailhead and Red Rock Passes are required (though they aren't available here).

A small sign at the north side of the parking lot points the way to the *Bell Rock* trail, a major trail that provides a stroll between Sedona and *Bell Rock*. It is best to ignore this sign and instead find a smaller trail that begins from about 20 yards south of the northern edge of the parking lot. This trail heads east and crosses the *Bell Rock* trail after 30 yards, where the latter trail follows a set of powerlines. The approach trail jogs 10 yards left here along the *Bell Rock* trail before it heads off east again at an open area by the powerlines. The approach trail is not marked, but it is worth taking the time to find, as it offers quick passage across the brushy lower slopes of the approach.

Follow this trail across relatively flat country toward the buttress for about 0.5 mile to an open area of slickrock. Trails branch here to north and south, but you want to head cross-country here up the ridge straight ahead that leads directly up to the rock. This ridge reaches the wall at a buttress a short way south of the left skyline buttress that houses the route. Hike up the progressively steepening ridge, picking your way through the fire-scarred, brushy vegetation and trees along discontinuous open areas. Stay on the ridge crest, which becomes easier to discern the higher you go. When you reach the base of the wall move left into the small drainage and up to the left skyline prow. The route begins on a ledge at the base of the straight-in corner system about 30 feet right of the prow.

FOUR FLYING APACHES (AKA GIBRALTAR or SEDONA SCENIC ROUTE), GRADE III 5.9 ★★★

FA: John Burcham 2001

This route tackles the impressive prow of Coconino Sandstone that looms to the east above the southern reaches of Sedona between Chapel of the Holy Cross and *Bell Rock*. The prow is awesome from a distance but looks more ragged as you examine it from closer range. This route scours the complex topography around the prow in search of quality climbing and, amazingly, finds it. The route is so new that it hasn't appeared in any previous guidebooks, but it is already the subject of big word-of-mouth and Internet buzz, and deservedly so. It is representative of modern Sedona neoclassics, which employ many more bolts than

Jamming the initial moves on Four Flying Apaches

earlier climbs in order to safely traverse some of the area's beautiful faces and link otherwise isolated sections of elegant crack climbing. Few first ascensionists have invested more money and effort to make a route safe and enjoyable than John Burcham has here. The result is a series of five beautiful and varied pitches that take you up the prow of a striking wall high above Sedona with magnificent views of many of the area's famous rocks, including *The Mace, Streaker Spire,* and *Bell Rock.*

Pitch One: Ascend the straight-in corner to a light-colored roof. Turn the roof on the left via liebacks. The crack behind the roof is too wide for conventional pro, but a smaller crack right below the roof provides good protection for this crux move. Continue up the crack above and left of the roof to a huge belay ledge with a double-bolt anchor. 5.8+, 130 feet.

Pitch Two: Before doing this pitch, shift the belay about 30 feet right to a small but good belay ledge equipped with a double-bolt belay/rappel anchor with chains, or to the much larger ledge with the pine tree just above. From either ledge move up the white, bolt-studded face above. The bolts continually lead you to the left onto steeper face climbing, avoiding the easy groove immediately to the right. Above the fifth bolt the route finally gives up and steps right onto the easy ground above the groove. The sixth bolt is actually a double bolt (which can be used as the anchor for an additional rappel if you are descending with 50-meter ropes). From it move up and right, past one more bolt, to a comfortable double-bolt belay at the base of an impressive off-width crack that splits the steep wall above. 5.7, 110 feet. **Pitch Three:** Instead of climbing the obvious off-width, the route does an improbable-looking traverse across the steep wall to the left, past 2 bolts. A good crack protects the initial traverse moves to the first bolt. Above the second bolt the climbing eases as you move up a hand crack. The crack gets steeper, more difficult, and more aesthetic the higher you climb. It ends on a ledge below a short face with 1 bolt on it. Climb past this bolt to the large ledge above and belay from double bolts. As you move past the final bolt, take note of the double bolts with chains to your right, which form one of the anchors for the rappel. 5.8+, 140 feet. **Pitch Four:** Ascend the obvious line of bolts directly above the

belay to another ledge with a double-bolt anchor. Ten feet left of this belay anchor lies a chain-equipped triple-bolt anchor for the descent. Eight bolts protect this delicate, aesthetic face pitch. 5.8+, 100 feet. **Pitch Five:** Move right on exciting face moves with a crack for protection to an overhanging crack. This is the route's crux. Climb up this crack as it turns into a chimney. Ascend the chimney to the top of the buttress and belay from a bolted rappel anchor. 5.9, 100 feet. **Descent:** Rappel the route. It is best to have two 60-meter ropes, but you can get by with two 50-meter ropes if you make one additional rappel. From the top of pitch five, rappel with 2 ropes from the bolted anchor to the triple-bolt anchor just left of the belay anchor atop pitch four. From this triple-bolt anchor make a second double-rope rappel to the double bolts with chains that lie just right of the upper bolt mentioned in pitch three. If you have 60-meter ropes, do a third rappel from this anchor to the chain-equipped anchor at the base of pitch two (the ropes will just barely make it). If your ropes are shorter than this, stop at the double-bolt anchor that forms the sixth bolt on pitch two. There are no chains here so you'll need to leave a sling. From these bolts make a short fourth rappel down to the chains at the base of pitch two. Whichever way you reach the chain anchor at the base of pitch two, from it make a final 120-foot rappel to the ground.

Bell Rock

Approach: From the highway junction in downtown Sedona, travel 5.1 miles south on SR 179 to the large *Bell Rock* parking area on the left (east) side of the road at milepost 308.1. Red Rock parking passes are required. From the parking area hike south on the obvious and popular *Bell Rock* trail a few hundred yards until it becomes easy to scramble up onto the slickrock and into the amphitheater that faces west between the horseshoe-shaped arms of the *Bell Rock* massif. Scramble up this amphitheater along ever-steepening slickrock and take the right fork of the gully near the top to achieve the platform at the head of the amphitheater. This involves some exposed third-class scrambling. From the platform, move left (north) behind a small tower to a pass between the main rock and another tower. From the pass, move left on a ledge beneath the northeast face of the summit towers, just below the limestone band. The ledge ends beneath a notch between the two main towers. Look for an anchor bolt below an obvious weakness in the limestone band. The approach takes 15–20 minutes.

BELL ROCK 5.8 ★

FA: Bob Kamps and others 1957

It isn't every day that you can climb into a vortex, so don't pass up this wonderful opportunity! Sedona is an international nerve center for New Age spirituality, thanks to the eight vortices that lie among its beautiful red walls. These vortices are power centers, where the energy of the earth emanates from the ground. If you don't know about vortices and are curious, you can easily get an introductory education at one of the many New Age shops in Sedona. If you are a devotee, bring your crystals along; where else can you recharge them while you climb! The climb itself is an enjoyable, low-commitment way to introduce yourself to Sedona climbing; pretty much all the joys and horrors you'll find on other climbs are found here in miniature along its 100-foot length. The approach is short and unusually brush-free, but it is typically Sedona. Soft, loose rock, gritty cracks, and a scenic summit tower—it's all here and you can do it car to car in less time than it sometimes takes to get through a Sedona traffic jam. The route faces northeast.

From the anchor bolt move up through the weakness in the limestone band to a large ledge with a bush on it. Pass a bolt (which is intended as a belay anchor if you start the climb on this ledge) and tackle the obvious crack in the corner above. You can get good gear in this crack, but the crux is also protected by a hangerless bolt. Two hangerless bolts from the 1950s originally protected this section. When the bolts were replaced, it was decided to preserve some of the route's original flavor by leaving this bolt hangerless. It is a good hex-head bolt with a washer on it, so you can safely use it if you bring a keyhole hanger or sling it with a wired nut. If you bring Aliens or the like, the bolt isn't really even necessary for protection. After moving past the bolt you encounter easy ground above to the notch. Another hangerless bolt (this one with a wing nut!) has recently been installed here to replace the old piton that was originally used. The piton, a small piece of history, is still there. Move up and right to a crack under a roof. Two bolts (with hangers) protect these moves through a section of loose rock. Finish with a short crack that leads past the right side of the roof. Another bolt stud exists here, but it is useless (no hanger or nut). Pull onto the summit of the tower at a double-bolt belay anchor. Bring stoppers and cams, from small Aliens to a #2 Camalot. 5.8, 100 feet. **Descent:** Rappel the route from the double bolts on the summit. A 50-meter rope barely makes it back to the ledge at the start of the route.

Mars Attacks!

Approach: From the T-intersection in downtown Sedona travel west on SR 89A 3.4 miles to Dry Creek Road (at milepost 371). Turn right

MARS ATTACKS! APPROACH

2 ropes

2 ropes

approach

(north) onto this paved road and follow it 2 miles to a fork. The left, paved fork leads to Long and Boynton Canyon Roads. Take the right fork, Forest Road 152, toward Vultee Arch. This is a rough dirt road but is usually fine for two-wheel-drive vehicles. An automated vending machine dispensing Red Rocks parking passes is located here. Follow the dirt road for 1.3 miles to the Devil's Bridge trailhead, where you can easily see the route on the buttress to the left. Drive 0.25 mile past the Devil's Bridge trailhead to a small pullout on the left and park. Walk back down the road toward Devil's Bridge about 90 yards to a tall juniper that stands unusually close to the road on the left (east) side. A trail leads left (east) past this tree and up a small wash. A cairn usually marks the trail's start. The trail continues northeast up the wash toward the rock, with a few intermittent cairns marking the way. The trail aims for a breach in the prominent lower cliff band below the northwest face of the formation. More frequent cairns and a more obvious trail lead up the slope through this breach. Once through the cliff band the trail comes to a T-junction, with one branch leading left and the other right, traversing the vegetated slope below the main cliff. Take the right fork (going south), walking first beneath the narrow prow of the Fin and then beneath the southwest face. Where the *Mars Attacks!* buttress protrudes from the main wall, leave this good trail on a faint climber's trail that leads up the short slope beneath a low-angled slab left of the buttress. The climb begins at the left edge of this slab, and is marked by a line of bolts.

MARS ATTACKS! 5.8 ★★★

FA: John Burcham and others 2000

This is another John Burcham neoclassic. The climb dishes up just about every type of climbing in its four pitches. Two delicate friction pitches serve as bookends to a memorable horizontal face traverse along the limestone band and a wonderful, long pitch of crack climbing. The face pitches are well protected by bolts where the climbing is difficult, and the crack offers excellent protection. The route doesn't ascend a freestanding spire, but rather a piece of the mesa rim known as the Fin. It is a good idea to locate the climb from the Devil's Bridge trailhead before driving to the parking area. It tackles a prominent crack in a buttress that protrudes from the otherwise fairly smooth wall. A major right-facing corner (Big Corner) lies on the right side of this buttress. The climb faces southwest. It is helpful to bring two 60-meter ropes for the last pitch and the rappel.

Pitch One: Begin at the far left side of the low-angle slab and ascend

it past 5 bolts, angling right. The first bolt is very high off the ground. The climbing up to it is quite moderate, but the rock is soft so use caution. Once you clip the bolt, the climbing is well protected through a crux of pure friction climbing. Belay at 2 bolts on a ledge atop the limestone band. 5.8, 90 feet. **Pitch Two:** The memory of this pitch will stick with you for awhile! Traverse straight right, around the corner, along the limestone band past 6 bolts to a double-bolt belay at the base of the prominent crack that splits the buttress. The holds are good on the solid limestone rock and the air under your feet is exhilarating. Keep in mind that, because of its horizontal nature, the protection is about the same for the leader and the second climber on this pitch. 5.8, 85 feet. **Pitch Three:** Hustle up the crack, utilizing the abundant face holds to either side of it. The belay ledge lies off to the left of the crack and is marked by double bolts. Look for it before you reach the crack's end. The pitch swallows a lot of gear and it is a good idea to bring doubles of #1 to #3

Camalots and one #4. Many leaders may be happy to have a third #2 as well. 5.8, 130 feet. **Pitch Four:** Continue up the remainder of the crack to its end, then up the slab above past 2 bolts. Step left at a low-angle area to a second slab with 3 bolts. The angle eases above the last bolt, with no further protection on easy ground for 40 feet to a double-bolt belay on a ledge. 5.8, 170 feet. **Descent:** From the belay atop pitch four, move 40 feet right to a double-bolt rappel anchor with chains. The descent rappels the climb *Big Corner*, a large, right-facing dihedral, and requires 2 ropes. It can be done a variety of ways, depending on whether you have 60-meter ropes. By far the easiest and safest way down is with two 60-meter ropes. From the chain anchor rap down to a triple-bolt anchor at a tiny ledge on the face right of *Big Corner*. From the triple-bolt anchor rappel to the ground. *Note:* If you have 50- or 55-meter ropes, you can still get down, but it is more of a nuisance. There are several choices. The best option is to make the second rappel, off the triple bolts, to a double-bolt anchor at the top of pitch one of *Big Corner*. It is a little awkward to reach these bolts because you have to angle left at the end of the rap. From there you can easily reach the ground in a third rappel.

Kate McEwen airing it out on the wild limestone traverse pitch of Mars Attacks!

Oak Creek Overlook

The volcanic lands around Flagstaff provide numerous venues for stellar crack climbing on columnar basalt. The most famous of these areas is Paradise Forks. "The Forks," as it is known locally, is one of Arizona's premier climbing areas, but unfortunately its charms are largely lost on climbers who have yet to master the nuances of 5.10–5.11 crack climbing. But not to despair, Oak Creek Overlook provides basalt cracks every bit as clean and classic as the nearby Paradise Forks at more moderate grades. The Overlook provides several nice climbs in the 5.6 to 5.7 range and a plethora of outstanding 5.8 and 5.9 routes.

The Overlook's popularity is augmented by its close proximity to both Flagstaff and Sedona, as well as by its spectacular natural setting at the top of beautiful Oak Creek Canyon. Tourists come to the Overlook in droves to soak up the stunning view down into the canyon. The cliffs face south and are nestled in a forest of pine, juniper, and oak that provides shade for belayers on hot days.

The routes are all traditional, but the short approach, very close spacing between routes, and their 60- to 100-foot lengths make the area feel somewhat like a sport climbing venue. But unlike a sport climbing area, classic cracks are the order of the day here. The long, columnar basalt wall is complexly textured with cracks, corners, and roofs. The rock is steep and demands

Who doesn't enjoy a bowl of Duck Soup?

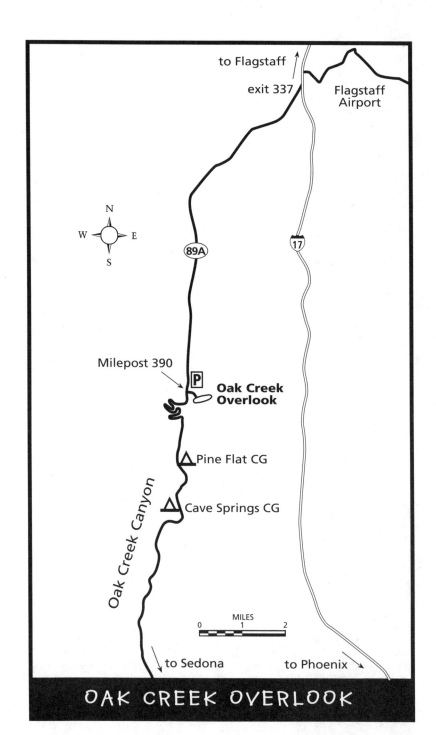

to Flagstaff

exit 337

Flagstaff Airport

N
W   E
S

89A

17

Milepost 390

P Oak Creek Overlook

Pine Flat CG

Cave Springs CG

Oak Creek Canyon

MILES
0   1   2

to Sedona

to Phoenix

OAK CREEK OVERLOOK

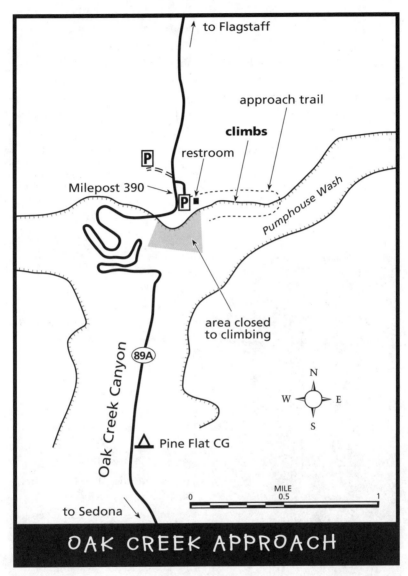

OAK CREEK APPROACH

excellent technique to avoid pumping yourself out. For climbers who revel in hand jams and stemming up aesthetic corners, this is your area. The smooth basalt is easy on the hands, unlike granite, so this is a great place to hone your crack climbing technique. And if you are not yet comfortable with the fine art of stemming, the Overlook is the place to experiment with this energy-saving technique; you'll be amazed at how much easier it makes many of the climbs here.

Most of the climbs here are fun leads that offer great protection, but if you want to top-rope, the tops of all climbs can be easily accessed from the rim. However, it is not advisable to set up a slingshot to belay from the base because the lip of the cliff is littered with loose rocks that could be dislodged by the unattended top rope. If you do want to top-rope climbs, belay from the top. Top anchors for most climbs consist of trees or slung blocks that sit back away from the rim; long slings can be handy to use these anchors.

A few noteworthy hazards of climbing at the Overlook are wasps and cacti. Many a climber has unwittingly grabbed a handful of cactus as he or she reached up blindly on a climb. Some of the ledges also host piles of mouse poop, which ordinarily is more unpleasant than hazardous; however, Hantavirus is carried by some mice in Arizona (although not to my knowledge at the Overlook), so it is best to avoid touching the stuff.

About half of the climbing at the Overlook was placed off-limits by the Forest Service in the mid 1990s due to concern that tourists, unaware of the climbing activities below, would hurl lethal objects down onto climbers. A number of fun moderate routes were lost to this closure, but fortunately the best section of wall remains open. The Northern Arizona Climbing Coalition and the Access Fund have been talking with the Forest Service in hopes of reopening these cliffs. If they succeed, it will double the number of routes available in the 5.6–5.9 range. In the meantime, there is plenty to keep you occupied for several weekends of fun.

The Overlook was first developed in the early 1970s as a practice area for the Flagstaff-based climbers of the Syndicato Granitica, whose

Charity Kahn soaks up the winter sun at Oak Creek Overlook. (Photo: Charlie Crocker)

Trinity Cracks area • Orange Out area • Burnt Tree Ledge area • Dugald's Right area • approach

OAK CREEK OVERLOOK OVERVIEW

members explored and developed many Arizona climbing areas in a prolific explosion of inspired activity. Although much of the first ascent history of individual lines at the Overlook was never written down, climbers such as Scott Baxter, Lee Dexter, Tom Tabor, and Karl Karlstrom were instrumental in the development of the area. Syndicato climbers were not prone to overrating their climbs, so expect to find full value for the grade on these climbs, as is the case at other Syndicato-developed areas such as Granite Mountain.

OAK CREEK OVERLOOK BETA

Drive time from Tucson	▲	4 hours
Drive time from Phoenix	▲	2 hours
Drive time from Flagstaff	▲	20 minutes

Getting there: Oak Creek Overlook is just 12 miles south of Flagstaff. From Flagstaff and points north, drive south on I-17 to exit 337, marked to the Flagstaff Airport and SR 89A to Oak Creek Canyon and Sedona. Drive 9 miles south on SR 89A to the scenic overlook sign at milepost 390. The Oak Creek scenic overlook is at the lip of the deep, spectacular Oak Creek Canyon, so if you miss the turn you will immediately begin dropping into the canyon on a series of switchback turns. Park in the Overlook parking area along with the hordes of sightseers. The gate into the parking lot is closed from approximately 5:30 PM to 8:00 AM (closure times are posted and vary seasonally), so if you think you will be climbing late (or if the gate is locked, as it usually is in the winter), park across the highway on a short dirt road. From Phoenix, Tucson, and other places to the south you have a choice. Either drive up I-17 to exit 337 and follow the directions above (the most efficient way) or take the scenic road through Sedona. For the latter, leave I-17 at exit 229 and follow SR 179 to Sedona. At the T-junction in downtown Sedona turn right onto SR 89A, which follows Oak Creek Canyon for 16 miles of slow, scenic road up to the Overlook just beyond milepost 390.

Approach: The approach entails an easy 10-minute walk from the parking lot. A short set of stairs leaves the east side of the parking area on the north side (away from the Overlook). A climber's trail begins here and crosses the flat ground above the cliffs. After less than 5 minutes of walking, the trail descends a short, steep slope around the east edge of the cliff band. From here the trail turns right and follows the base of the cliff to access the climbs. The first climbs you reach, after about 30 yards of walking along the base, are *Bush Rush* and *Griffo*. About 70 yards of additional walking place you beneath Burnt Tree Ledge, where several climbs begin, and about 25 yards farther you emerge from trees into an open area littered with broken boulders. This open area is the most distinctive landmark along the base of the wall, and the climbs in the Orange Out area ascend the cliff directly above it. Continuing about 50 yards beyond the far (west) side of the open area places you directly below the Trinity Cracks area, made immediately recognizable by the three beautiful 5.10 cracks that split the wall. *Red Wagon* and *Grunt 'n Dangle* begin just left of these cracks. The section of wall west of here is off-limits to climbing.

To descend, you can either walk back around to the base of the cliff following the approach route or bring an extra rope and leave a fixed rappel line from one of the stout junipers that line the top of the cliff. Most of these rappels are about 100 feet. Two commonly used rappels are down *Everyday Five-Three* and *Mint Julep*. The recent drought has killed or weakened many trees throughout the area, so pay close attention to the health of your proposed rappel anchor. Don't rappel from a dead tree no matter how large it is. Please make sure that nobody is climbing below you before you set up the rappel, and respect the desires of other climbers to ascend the route you have your rappel line on.

Season and Elevation: The 6400-foot elevation and south-facing aspect of this area make for comfortable year-round climbing. As with all Arizona climbing areas, spring and fall are best. It gets hot during the summer, but most of the climbs fall into shade by about 2:00 PM. On sunny winter days the southern exposure and black rock make for delightfully warm climbing.

Regulations: The Coconino National Forest, which manages the area, has closed off the section of cliff left of the Trinity Cracks area due to its location directly below an immensely popular tourist overlook. Please respect this closure.

Camping: Primitive, at-large camping is available on several dirt Forest Service roads 1–2 miles north of the Overlook off SR 89A. The nearest developed campground is Pine Flat, 3 miles south, down in Oak Creek Canyon. Flagstaff also has an abundance of cheap motels if you'd rather not camp.

Food and Supplies: Everything you could want is available 12 miles to the north in Flagstaff.

Gear: There is almost no fixed protection on these routes. Many routes devour multiple cams, especially in small to medium sizes, so augmenting a standard rack with a second set of cams is prudent. Stoppers and Aliens or other micro cams fit well in many of the thinner cracks. Many routes traverse around overhangs or switch crack systems, so you will want to have several long runners available to reduce rope drag. Bring along a spare rope to fix as a rappel line if you want to avoid walking around the east end of the cliff each time you top out on a route. Nearby Flagstaff hosts several outdoor stores if you find you are missing something you need.

Emergency Services: Flagstaff Medical Center is located at 1200 North Beaver Street in Flagstaff. (520-779-3366)

Kids and Dogs: The easy approach and the comfortable area around the base of the cliffs make this a good area for bringing the family, including canines on a leash.

1. RED WAGON 5.8 ★★

This route ascends a nice hand crack up a light gray wall left of the three prominent Trinity Cracks. Begin up easy, broken blocks that lead to the base of the crack, which begins with thin hands and widens as it goes up. Step left at the top of the crack to exit. This route swallows lots of cams in the #½–#2 Camalot range, so having doubles is wise. A #3 Camalot also comes in handy. 80 feet.

This climber contemplates his next move on Red Wagon.

2. GRUNT 'N DANGLE 5.7
★★

There is really no need to grunt or dangle on this fun route. Are you interested in an off-width that you protect with wired stoppers? Then this is the route for you. Ascend easy, broken blocks to the off-width crack in the right-facing dihedral immediately left of the Trinity Cracks. A thin crack just to the right provides good holds and protection. At the top of the crack traverse to the right above the Trinity Cracks and below an overhang on a series of ledges. Turn the overhang on its right side via exhilarating moves, then scamper to the top. It is important to use long slings on gear for the traverse to avoid nasty rope drag. A standard rack protects this route. 110 feet.

TRINITY CRACKS AREA

The Trinity Cracks

1

2

Note: The three Trinity Cracks are all outstanding climbs, with the left crack checking in at 5.10a, the middle crack at 5.10c, and the right crack at 5.10b.

3. ISAIAH 5.9 ★★★

A good workout is guaranteed with any ascent of this outstanding hand crack. It simultaneously demands arm strength and finesse. A prominent, right-arching hand crack cuts the steep face around the corner to the right from the Trinity Cracks. Begin on *Mint Jam* and cut left to the base of *Isaiah* when you reach the top of the block. Ascend

the crack, which widens after a cruxy, thin hands start, through a small overhang to the top. It is handy to have doubles on Camalots ranging from #½–#1 for protection. 100 feet.

4. MINT JAM 5.7 ★★

This enjoyable route ascends the hand crack in a corner 30 feet right of the prominent Trinity Cracks. A 20-foot-tall block with a ledge on top protrudes from the lower portion of the buttress. Begin just left

EVERYDAY FIVE-THREE

⑤

of a tall juniper and ascend the inside corner that forms the right side of this block to the ledge on its top. Continue up the double hand crack directly above the ledge to the top. The route protects well with doubles of #2–#3 Camalots. 100 feet.

5. EVERYDAY FIVE-THREE 5.6 ★★

This chimney offers a pleasant change of pace from the normal Oak Creek Overlook climb. Begin about 100 feet left of the open area at the base of the cliff, where the trail squeezes between a fallen boulder and a small stump. Begin climbing up the crack that rises above the boulder, immediately right of a tall pine tree that grows next to the wall. The crack leads to a ledge about 30 feet up. Enter the depths of the chimney that looms above the ledge. Good holds and cracks line its walls. Wriggle past some blocks that plug the top of the chimney, and exit to the right on steep rock with good holds. 100 feet.

6. GINGERBREAD 5.7 ★★★

This very enjoyable climb keeps you on your toes through three crux sections separated by excellent rests. Begin at a section of broken rock that lies about 60 feet right of the Trinity Cracks and 90 feet left of the open boulder field mentioned in the approach description. Ascend a

GINGERBREAD AREA

crack in the left side of the broken rock to a black roof about 15 feet off the ground. Turn the roof on the left to a ledge beneath beautiful double hand cracks. Stem up the cracks to another ledge. Beware of cacti as you pull up onto this ledge. Step left and ascend steep, broken blocks to a large juniper on the rim. This is the juniper mentioned as a good rappel anchor in the approach description. 100 feet.

7. ANGEL'S DELIGHT 5.8 ★★★

This route delivers continuously excellent climbing. Begin 10 feet right of *Gingerbread* at an inside corner that marks the right side of a broken area of black rock. Ascend the corner, which becomes progressively more difficult, to the base of a knife-edged arête. Move right into a right-angling corner crack. The crack splits a short distance above, with the left fork shooting straight up through bulging rock. Take the lower-angled right fork into a deep, shady corner. Ascend this corner beneath a roof and hand traverse around it to the right, using good cracks. These cracks take you to a blunt arête, which you ascend to the top. Bring cams up to a #3 Camalot. 110 feet.

8. AMATEUR HOUR 5.9 ★★★

Begin this wonderful route by climbing the first 20 feet of *Alley Oop* to the detached block. Move left just below the block up into a thin hand crack in a corner. Continue up this crack to a triangular overhang near the top. Turn the overhang on the left via good holds. The route takes doubles in #½–#1 Camalots along with a standard rack. 100 feet.

9. ALLEY OOP 5.7 ★★★

This is another outstanding route. Begin about 50 feet left of the open area mentioned in the approach description at a corner that rises just right of a large oak tree with two trunks that is missing its top and that grows very close to the wall. Either belay from this tree or scramble easily up the broken rock above for 20 feet to the base of the dihedral. Ascend the dihedral for 20 feet to a detached block. Turn the block on the right and continue up the maze of cracks that lies in the dihedral above, on the left side of a red slab. A lichen-covered headwall at the top can be turned either left or right, with the left exit considerably more difficult. Bring gear up to a #3 Camalot, with a double #¾ useful. 100 feet.

10. SYZYGY 5.8 ★★

This very nice route climbs up to a square, black roof at mid-height on the cliff. Begin the route about 20 feet left of the open area covered in boulders, beneath a broken gully that leads up to a ledge with a tree beneath the roof. You can scramble up to the ledge to belay or belay from the ground. Head up the dihedral to a stance under the roof. Turn the roof on its left side to a beautiful finger and hand crack above. 70 feet.

SYZYGY AREA

11. APPLESTICKS 5.8 ★

Climb *Syzygy* to the black roof, but turn the roof on the right instead of the left. Continue up the crack system above the roof, which soon peters out into thin seams. The crux involves doing some delicate face moves past these seams. Aliens and small stoppers are useful. 70 feet.

12. NORMALLY URGENT 5.8 ★★

The lower portion of this route involves some loose rock, but your reward is beautiful jamming up a hand crack that splits the clean, red slab above. Begin 6 feet left of *Morning's Mourning* at a face split by a vertical seam. Either climb this seam until it is possible to step into a wider crack 2 feet to the left or begin directly in this wider crack (though its base is guarded by sticker-covered bushes). Continue up this crack (#3 Camalot) and step gingerly left at its top onto a ledge strewn with rubble, cacti, and an agave. Reach the right-facing corner directly above the ledge via some dubious-sounding flakes. Ascend the corner as it arches left and

GINGERBREAD TO ORANGE
OUT DIRECT OVERVIEW

step left to reach the base of the hand crack splitting the distinctive red slab. Ascend this crack and the corners above to the top. The route takes a double set of #½–#1 Camalots. 100 feet.

13. MORNING'S MOURNING 5.8 ★★★

This is one of the best routes on the cliff. It tackles the obvious, clean, right-facing dihedral that rises above the left side of the open area at the cliff's base. Start in a left-leaning corner that leads up to broken rock below the right-facing dihedral and then climb it. Double cams up to #2 Camalot can be useful, as well as one #3. 100 feet.

14. MINT JULEP 5.9 ★★

The upper dihedral of this route offers some exquisite liebacking and stemming. Ascend broken, easy rock 5 feet right of the initial *Morning's Mourning* dihedral for about 30 feet to a section of steeper, broken rock above. You are aiming for the shallow, right-facing dihedral above that is immediately right of the larger *Morning's Mourning* dihedral. Move through this steeper rock, using Aliens or other thin crack gear for protection to reach the bottom of the shallow dihedral. An alternative start is to ascend *Morning's Mourning* to the base of its upper dihedral and traverse right on ledges. Climb the shallow dihedral via wonderful finger locks.

The crux comes right at the top, just before this climb merges with *Morning's Mourning*. Bring lots of stoppers and small cams. 100 feet.

15. ORANGE OUT DIRECT 5.9 ★★★

The finish of this stellar route up an overhanging slot will really stand out in your memory. This distinctive slot is easy to identify. Begin in an easy crack system 8 feet left of a large juniper growing out of the base of the rock on the right side of the open area. Ascend these cracks and the hand crack above to a short bulge below the black, overhanging slot. Turn the bulge to a rest stance at the base of the slot. You can place great gear from this stance. When you are ready, begin the exciting stemming that

Chance Traub ensures he stays wedged in the spectacular, overhanging final slot on Orange Out Direct.

leads up the slot to the top. In addition to a standard rack, this route takes double cams up to a #2 Camalot, and three #1 Camalots can come in handy. 100 feet.

16. CRACKUP 5.9- ★★★

This enjoyable, blocky crack splits the dark, clean face above Burnt Tree Ledge. The skeleton of the old, burnt tree standing on a ledge 30 feet up the wall is the most distinctive landmark in this section of cliff, which lies about 80 feet right of the open area beneath *Orange Out Direct*. Begin by scrambling up easy rock directly below the burnt tree to the ledge. *Crackup* tackles the crack immediately left of the tree. The crux is found in the final moves. Beware of wasps. This route takes lots of small gear up to a #1 Camalot. 60 feet.

17. BURNT BUNS 5.8 ★★★

This is just another high-quality crack route. Scramble up to Burnt Tree Ledge as described for *Crackup*. *Burnt Buns* ascends the crack and

corner system immediately right of the burnt tree. You will appreciate having a double set of #½–#2 Camalots, though many protection possibilities exist. 60 feet.

18. DUCK SOUP 5.6 ★★★

This is the best 5.6 at the Overlook, but it is far from trivial. This route ascends the double crack system that splits the face immediately right of Burnt Tree Ledge. Begin below and right of the ledge and ascend the cracks to the top. A standard rack protects the climb well, but there are options for placing a #3 Camalot. 80 feet.

19. DUGALD'S RIGHT 5.9 ★★

This is an enjoyable route that is considerably better than it appears from below. The route lies on the west side of the first prominent buttress the trail goes around on the approach as you traverse the base of the cliff. It is situated about 160 feet right of Burnt Tree Ledge. The route ascends cracks to the right side of a long, narrow roof about 15 feet off the ground. Turn the roof using cracks that cut its right side and continue to the top up the same crack system. Beware of wasps. Doubles of #¾–#2 Camalots are useful. 60 feet.

20. NORMALLY THREE RURPS 5.6 ★

This is probably the easiest route on the cliff. It begins about 60 feet left of *Bush Rush*, on the west side of the buttress mentioned in *Dugald's Right*. A series of cracks leads up the wall 3 feet right of the *Dugald's Right* roof. Go up these cracks, which lead around the corner to the right. When you reach an area of broken ledges go up a straight-in

DUGALD'S
RIGHT AREA

corner, step right at its end, and head up a second straight-in corner to the top. 60 feet.

21. BUSH RUSH 5.8 ★★

This is the first really obvious climb you reach as you approach the cliff. About 100 feet beyond the beginning of the cliff-base traverse you see a prominent and attractive thin hand crack that splits an orange wall. *Bush Rush* ascends this crack. 45 feet.

22. GRIFFO 5.6 ★★

This is the obvious crack immediately right of *Bush Rush*. Begin at a pointed boulder and climb a short face to gain the crack. Climb it to the top. 45 feet.

Lisa Campbell pulls on solid basalt at Oak Creek Overlook.

Jacks Canyon

Jacks Canyon is the biggest and most popular sport-climbing venue in northern Arizona. Its limestone walls host more than 200 well-protected, bolted face climbs up to a half pitch in length. The very fast and easy approach, the close spacing between routes, and the abundance of top anchors make this a place where visitors can tick off a lot of climbs in a weekend. Jacks offers fun, steep face climbing on pockets and small edges with plenty of bolts. There are a handful of nice crack climbs here, and even they are bolted! The area is also well-known for its soft ratings, so it is a good place to stroke your ego if you want to try for some big numbers. Unless otherwise noted in the route descriptions, you will probably find these climbs easy for the listed grade, provided you use your feet well and have good arm strength. Given the steep angle of the rock, Jacks climbing can be very strenuous, and you may find yourself getting pumped quickly.

The area lies on national forest land amidst pinyon–juniper woodland south of Winslow. A convenient camping area lies on the canyon rim just a short hike from the climbs. It used to offer pleasant, shaded camping spots, but the recent drought has killed most of the trees. The camping is still low-key; it just isn't as scenic as it once was.

Jacks is more remote than many of the areas listed in this guide. Make sure you don't forget any necessary gear or provisions, as

Kate McEwen shows she does indeed know Jack on You Don't Know Jack @#*!

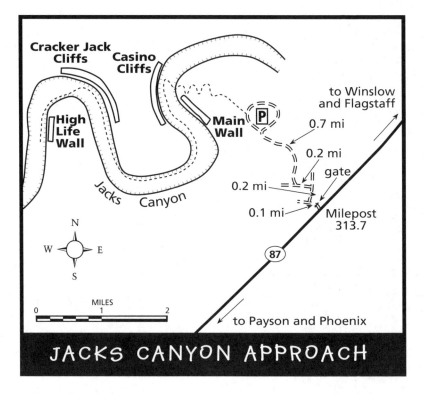

Cracker Jack Cliffs

Casino Cliffs

High Life Wall

Main Wall

P

to Winslow and Flagstaff

0.7 mi

0.2 mi

gate

0.2 mi

0.1 mi

Milepost 313.7

Jacks Canyon

87

N
W — E
S

MILES
0   1   2

to Payson and Phoenix

JACKS CANYON APPROACH

it is a long trek anywhere to get them. There is no water available in the area, so bring plenty with you. The secluded nature of this small canyon draining Arizona's Mogollon Rim kept it unknown to climbers until the early 1990s. It didn't take long, though, for people to realize that this was an area with the potential for hundreds of routes at all grades. A frenzy of new route activity ensued over the next decade, resulting in development of the quintessential sport crag. With exceptionally convenient climbing, a year-round season, and a low-key, relaxed atmosphere, Jacks is a place to enjoy the casual side of climbing.

JACKS CANYON BETA

Drive time from Tucson ▲ 4 hours

Drive time from Phoenix ▲ 2½ hours

Drive time from Flagstaff ▲ 1½ hours

Getting there: From Flagstaff take I-40 to Winslow (exit 253—North Park Drive) and continue south approximately 1 mile to Second Street.

Turn left, drive several blocks to the traffic light, then turn right (south), and you will be on SR 87 headed toward Payson. Continue south on this road about 30 miles to milepost 313.7. Turn right onto a dirt road and head through the gate (please close the gate behind you). From here, follow the road 0.1 mile and turn right. Go another 0.2 mile and turn left, then another 0.2 mile and turn right. From here, follow the road 0.7 mile to parking, camping, and the trailhead into the canyon. All these turns sound confusing, but they all keep you on the main dirt road at junctions with smaller, rougher roads.

From Phoenix, take I-17 north to Camp Verde and SR 260. Travel east on SR 260 until it dead-ends into SR 87. Turn left and follow SR 87 to mile marker 313.7. Turn left and go through the gate (please close it behind you) and follow the directions above. If you are in Mesa, Scottsdale, or Tucson, it is more efficient to follow SR 87 to Payson and Strawberry instead of taking I-17 north. This route joins the description from Phoenix at the SR 87/260 junction.

Approach: 5–15 minutes. A trail leads directly from the middle of the parking lot/camping area to the canyon rim and a short switchback descent into the canyon itself at the Casino Cliffs.

Season and Elevation: The area's 6200-foot elevation and the variety of orientations of the climbs ensure comfortable climbing year-round, but expect chilly camping in the winter. Summer days can be hot.

Regulations: The land here is part of the Coconino National Forest. The climbing area is closed to new route development. Contact the Access Fund for more information. At present there are no other specific regulations pertaining to climbing.

Camping: At-large camping is available at the parking lot. A toilet provides the only facilities. There is no water, so bring plenty with you. Please help keep access open in this area by cleaning up after yourself.

Food and Supplies: The nearest supplies are in Winslow, 30 miles to the northeast, where you will find an ample selection of grocery stores and fast food restaurants.

Gear: All of the climbing at Jacks Canyon is protected by bolts. A rack of 10 quickdraws will get you up anything here. Double-bolt or cold-shut anchors provide quick descents from all climbs. Each route description includes the number of bolts on the line. These bolt counts don't include the top anchors. While the route developers here have not skimped on bolt placements, they have chosen to place the first bolt on some climbs uncomfortably high for people who don't use a cheater stick. Many Jacks climbers bring a stick with them. I never have, but sometimes having a spotter is handy while getting to the first bolt.

Emergency Services: The nearest medical facilities are in Winslow at the Winslow Memorial Hospital, 1501 N. Williamson Ave. (928-289-4691)

Kids and Dogs: An easy approach and camping convenient to the climbing area make this a good place for kids and dogs on leashes.

Casino Cliffs

The Casino Cliffs is the first cliff band you reach as you descend into the gorge. It lies directly across the creek from the spot where the trail first descends into the canyon. The routes here face east, so they get good morning sun for winter climbing and nice, late-day shade during

Alison Kopinto steps out on Step Right Up *on the Cracker Jack Cliffs.*

CASINO CLIFFS
EDGE YOUR
BETS AREA

the warmer months. The access trail meets the cliff at the bottom of *Mickey Goes to Vegas*. A trail runs along the base of the cliff, offering easy access to all climbs. Although the first climb you get to is in the middle of the cliff, the climbs are numbered from far left to right. The route descriptions below should help to orient you from the base of *Mickey Goes to Vegas*, and help you to avoid inadvertently hopping on one of the many bolt lines not mentioned here, all of which are 5.10 and above.

Edge Your Bets and *Slots O Fun* are 40 feet left and uphill from *Double or Nothin'* on the obvious pocketed face.

1. EDGE YOUR BETS 5.10a ★★
FA: Deidre Burton 1995

This climb lies on a distinctive pocketed wall at the very left (south) end of the Casino Cliffs. It is the left of 2 bolt lines up the face. 4 bolts.

CASINO CLIFFS
BET ON BLACK
AREA

2. SLOTS O FUN 5.10a ★★★
FA: Deidre Burton 1995

This strenuous line has you pulling on the numerous pockets that stud the right side of the face listed in *Edge Your Bets*. Great climbing. 4 bolts.

Double or Nothin' and *Bet on Black* are on the narrow face located left up the hill and past a blocky rock from *Sports Book*.

3. DOUBLE OR NOTHIN' 5.9
FA: Matt Engbring 1996

This climb ascends the small spire formed by the left wall of a prominent dihedral that splits a buttress 40 feet right of the *Edge Your Bets* wall. The climbing is pleasant but somewhat contrived. 4 bolts.

4. BET ON BLACK 5.9 ★
FA: Jim Steagall

This route begins by ascending the lower portion of the dihedral mentioned in *Double or Nothin'*, then veers out onto the wall to the right. 6 bolts.

5. SPORTS BOOK 5.10a ★★★
FA: Brian Fife 1995

This prominent, bolted crack between two bulging overhangs provides beautiful stemming up a shallow corner that splits the cliff band 40 feet left of *Easy Money*. This climb is rated about right, with the crux near the bottom. 7 bolts.

6. EASY MONEY 5.7 ★
FA: Chris Hahn 1995

This lies on the face of a pillar that forms the left side of a distinctive right-facing dihedral immediately left of *Circus Circus*. An obvious gully lies on the left side of the same pillar. Ascend the dihedral using liebacks to the first bolt, then boldly tackle the pillar's steep face. 4 bolts.

7. CIRCUS CIRCUS 5.6 ★★
FA: Jim Steagall 1995

This route is 50 feet left of *Dealer's Choice*. It ascends the face on the right side of the dihedral described in *Easy Money*. An awkward struggle up the beginning of the dihedral yields to stellar climbing on positive holds up the gray face to anchor bolts in a distinctive white band. 5 bolts.

CASINO CLIFFS
SPORTS BOOK

8. DEALER'S CHOICE 5.10a ★★★

FA: Deidre Burton 1996

This climb is located 30 feet right of *Circus Circus* and 15 feet left of *Mickey Goes to Vegas*. It is hard to take this route's 5.10c rating in *Jacks Canyon Sport Climbing* by Burton and Steagall (see Appendix) seriously, but it is a great route all the same! Climb the small, right-facing corner situated a few feet left of the spot where the access trail meets the cliff.

Exhilarating liebacking and stemming offer a welcome change of pace from the standard Jacks face climb. 6 bolts.

9. MICKEY GOES TO VEGAS 5.9 ★★★
FA: Brian Fife 1995

It is hard to beat this route for sheer excitement. The route is directly in front of you where the access trail meets the cliff. A series of flakes leads up to a roof that sports a series of huecos in the shape of a Mouseketeer hat. Turn the roof on big jugs, then finish it on easier ground. 6 bolts.

10. FIST FULL O DOLLARS 5.10a ★
FA: Matt Engbring 1996

About 40 feet right of *Mickey Goes to Vegas* the cliff is broken by a deep chimney. This route tackles the arête immediately right of that chimney. 4 bolts.

11. UNKNOWN 5.4 ★★

This fun, moderate route ascends a series of small, left-facing dihedrals in a large white patch of rock. This route is well protected and makes a great first lead. 4 bolts.

CASINO CLIFFS MICKEY GOES TO VEGAS AREA

12. PROGRESSIVE SLOTS 5.6 ★★
FA: Jim Steagall 1996
This is the next line of bolts, about 15 feet right of the previous unknown climb. Surprisingly difficult climbing leads past the first bolt, but after that the route settles down to some steep, enjoyable climbing on big holds. 6 bolts.

13. ONE ARMED BANDIT 5.10a ★★
FA: Jim Steagall 1996
About 40 feet right of *Progressive Slots* the cliff is broken by another deep chimney. This is another fine arête climb immediately right of the chimney and left of a white patch. 5 bolts.

14. LET IT RIDE 5.9 ★
FA: Jim Steagall 1995
This is the next line of bolts right of *One Armed Bandit*, a shallow dihedral just right of a prominent white patch. The crux consists of the bouldery start. Easier climbing leads up the right-angling groove. 6 bolts.

15. MAVERICK 5.9 ★
FA: Deidre Burton 1995
This is the fourth line of bolts right of *Let it Ride* (the first bolt is immediately right of a white streak). You have to scramble up over a

few boulders at the base of the cliff to reach this line, which provides another surprisingly tricky crux low down that yields to easier moves above. 3 bolts.

16. ANTE UP 5.8 ★★
FA: Deidre Burton 1995
This is the rightmost line on the cliff. Start immediately right of *Maverick*, just to the climber's right of a large tree, and ascend nice, black rock to the top. 3 bolts.

Cracker Jack Cliffs

To reach this wall hike upstream on the obvious trail from the left side of Casino Cliffs and around a sweeping bend of the wash to the right. In about 5 minutes of walking, you reach the Cracker Jack Cliffs, where the rock on your right becomes tall enough to warrant roped climbing. Climbs on the cliff are listed from left to right, but you will approach the right-hand climbs first. The Cracker Jack Cliffs continue around the next sweeping

McNeill Mann enjoys the latest Best Seller.

bend of the wash (this one to the left), so they offer south-facing climbs on the left side and west-facing climbs on the right. This variety makes these cliffs an ideal place to capture winter sun or summer shade.

1. BIG PLANS 5.10a ★
FA: Deidre Burton 1996
You'll find this climb near the far left side of the wall, just past a tree whose trunk hugs the ground as it grows straight out from the wall. Liebacking gets you past the crux right off the ground, then yields to some pleasant stemming and crack moves. 5 bolts.

2. BEST SELLER 5.9 ★★★
FA: Jim Steagall 1996
This outstanding stemming corner provides wonderful climbing. It lies 50 feet right of *Big Plans*, behind a large boulder and right of a large, obvious roof high on the cliff. 6 bolts.

3. JACK FROST 5.9 ★★
FA: Brett Clarkson 1996
A bulge low down forms the crux on this nice route that takes the left of 2 bolt lines on a narrow buttress 80 feet right of *Best Seller*. 4 bolts.

CRACKER JACK CLIFFS
BIG PLANS AND BEST SELLER

Michael Nemeth hits the Jack Pot.

4. JACK POT 5.8 ★
FA: Brett Clarkson 1996

This is the right bolt line on the narrow buttress. The crux comes as you move up to clip the second bolt. There is a ground-fall potential here, so use caution. 4 bolts.

5. JACK OFF 5.8 ★★
FA: Brett Clarkson 1996

This fun route takes the bolt line up the extreme left side of the broader buttress 30 feet right of the *Jack Frost* buttress. The rock bulges here but is studded with lots of friendly huecos. 4 bolts.

Wendy Parkinson powers over the initial bulge on Jack Off.

6. UNKNOWN 5.9 ★★

This route takes the line of bolts just a few feet right of *Jack Off*, up smooth, clean rock with a thin crack splitting it. The climbing is truly elegant. 5 bolts.

7. CHARLIE DON'T SEND 5.9 R ★

FA: Brett Clarkson 1996

This route takes the third line of bolts right of *Jack Off*, up the far right side of the broad buttress. Thin, bulgy moves lead to the first bolt (easier if you come in from the right), then the difficulty eases until you reach the strenuous bulge near the top. *Jacks Canyon Sport Climbing* by Burton and Steagall (see Appendix) shows a fifth bolt after the bulge, but it is missing, making the easy upper moves run out. Use caution clipping the anchors. 4 bolts.

8. JACK'S CROWN 5.10a ★
FA: Deidre Burton 1996

A gully separates the *Jack Off* buttress from a much longer cliff band on the right. A large clump of trees stands at the base of this long cliff band. *Jack's Crown* takes the furthest left line of bolts on this cliff, immediately right of the gully. The climbing is enjoyable but doesn't rise to 5.10a difficulty. The farther left you move, the easier it gets. 4 bolts.

9. JILL AND DRILL 5.10a ★★
FA: Deidre Burton 1996

This enjoyable route takes the first line of bolts right of *Jack's*

Laura Plaut contemplates the bulge on Charlie Don't Send.

CRACKER JACK CLIFFS JACK FROST TO CHARLIE DON'T SEND

CRACKER JACK CLIFFS JILL AND DRILL AREA

Crown, to an anchor right of the prominent white roof capping the cliff. 5 bolts.

Climbs 10–16 lie 300 feet to the right (east) of the previously described climbs. The most obvious landmark is the 40-foot-high Sinker Boulder (see climb 15) that sits between the cliff wall and the creek.

10. BETTY CRACKER 5.9 ★★
FA: Deidre Burton 1996

This is the bolt line immediately left of *You Don't Know Jack @#*!*. Ascend a prominent crack–dihedral with bolts on its right side to a small roof, then continue up the face. 5 bolts.

Alison Kopinto establishes herself in the crack of Betty Cracker.

CRACKER JACK CLIFFS SINKER AREA OVERVIEW

11. YOU DON'T KNOW JACK @#*! 5.9 ★★★

FA: Deidre Burton 1996

Immediately behind the distinctive boulder that hosts *Sinker*, the main wall is cleaved by a prominent chimney. This route is the bolt line immediately left of the chimney. It ascends the wonderful pocketed wall and turns a small roof near the top. 4 bolts.

12. STEP RIGHT UP 5.9 ★

FA: Jim Steagall 1996

This is the first bolt line right of the large chimney described in the previous route. Interesting climbing leads up a smooth face that is less textured than the average Jacks wall. 3 bolts.

13. SNAP, CRACK OR POP 5.9 ★

FA: Jim Steagall 1996

This is the bolt line immediately right of *Step Right Up*, 15 feet right of the chimney. Surprisingly delicate moves lead up the steep face. 3 bolts.

14. JACKSON FIVE TEN 5.10a ★★

FA: Jim Steagall 1996

This is the next bolt line right of *Snap, Crack, or Pop*. It is located just left of a large roof 10 feet off the ground, and immediately behind a juniper. Move left around the roof and up the face. 5 bolts.

McNeill Mann stepping up to the climbing on Step Right Up

15. SINKER 5.5 ★★★

FA: Chris Hahn 1996

This unusual route lies on an obvious, massive talus block that has lodged itself below the main cliff on the bank of the creek. Begin on the boulder's right side. If the water is high, a delicate dance is required to get on the rock without getting your shoes wet. The route angles up and left to the top. 5 bolts.

16. SAUCY JACK 5.10a ★★

FA: Jim Steagall 1996

Right of the prominent low roof mentioned in *Jackson Five Ten* is a blocky buttress with a small talus pile built up below its right side. Three bolt lines stud this buttress. *Saucy Jack* takes the rightmost of these bolt lines, up a blunt arête. Easy climbing down low yields to more difficult moves up and left to the anchors. 4 bolts.

CRACKER JACK CLIFFS SNAP CRACK POP AREA

High Life Wall

From the Cracker Jack area, cross the river and continue upstream for about 5 minutes to the west-facing High Life Wall. This wall is composed of unusually white, sandy rock that is more finger friendly than most Jacks rock. The routes are moderate, they feel easier than their grades suggest, and the bolts are abundant and well placed. This is the best beginner's wall at Jacks. These routes hold nice afternoon sun.

1. WALK IN THE PARK 5.9 ★★
FA: Chris Hahn 1996
This is the leftmost bolt line. A crux bulge getting off the ground leads to more moderate climbing above. The middle of the route follows a low-angle crack. 6 bolts.

2. LOOKING SHARP 5.8 ★★★
FA: Chris Hahn 1996
The middle route on the wall is the best beginner's climb at Jacks.

HIGH LIFE WALL

The rock is friendly and the bolt placements are excellent, making this a good choice for people wanting to break into leading. 6 bolts.

3. SUNDAY STROLL 5.8 ★★
FA: Chris Hahn 1996

This is the longest route on the wall. Climb the rightmost line of bolts. The climbing is moderate until the rock steepens around the last bolt. 7 bolts.

Appendixes

A. ADDITIONAL RESOURCES AND LAND MANAGEMENT INFORMATION

Cochise Stronghold
Coronado National Forest
Cochise Ranger Station, Douglas Ranger District Office
(520) 378-0311

Kerry, Bob. *Backcountry Rockclimbing in Southern Arizona*. Tucson, AZ:
  Backcountry Enterprises LLC, 1997.

Granite Mountain
Prescott National Forest
344 South Cortez St., Prescott, AZ 86303
(928) 443-8000, TTY (928) 443-8001; *www.fs.fed.us/r3/prescott*

Green, Stewart M. *Rockclimbing Arizona*. Helena, MT: Falcon Press, 1999.
Waugh, Jim. "An Updated Topo Guide to Granite Mountain," *Rock and
  Ice* #24, March/April 1988.

Jacks Canyon
Coconino National Forest
Mogollon Rim Ranger District
(928) 477-2255; *www.fs.fed.us/r3/coconino*

Burton, Deidre and Jim Steagall. *Jacks Canyon Sport Climbing*.
  Self-published, 1999.

McDowell Mountains
McDowell Sonoran Preserve
(480) 312-7722; *www.ci.scottsdale.az.us/preserve*

Karabin, Marty. *McDowell Mountains North Scottsdale Rock Climbing and
  Hiking Guide*. Phoenix, AZ: MK Productions, 1996.
Opland, Greg. *Phoenix Rock II*. Evergreen, CO: Chockstone Press, 1996.

Mount Lemmon
Coronado National Forest
Santa Catalina Ranger District
520-749-8700, *www.fs.fed.us/r3/coronado/scrd/rec/rockclimb/rockclimbing.htm*

Fazio-Rhicard, Eric. *Squeezing the Lemmon II: A Rock Climber's Guide to the Mount Lemmon Highway.* Tucson, AZ: E Squared Enterprises, 2000.

Oak Creek Overlook
Coconino National Forest
Mormon Lake Ranger District
(928) 774-1147; *www.fs.fed.us/r3/coconino*

Green, Stewart M. *Rockclimbing Arizona.* Helena, MT: Falcon Press, 1999.
Karabin, Marty. *The Overlook: Oak Creek Canyon, Arizona.* Phoenix, AZ: MK Productions, 2003.
Toula, Tim. *A Cheap Way to Fly: Free Climbing Guide to Northern Arizona.* Lander, WY: Little Wanderer Publishing, 1991.

Pinnacle Peak
City of Scottsdale Pinnacle Peak Park
26802 N. 102nd Way
Scottsdale, AZ 85255
(480) 312-0990; *jloleit@ScottsdaleAZ.gov; www.ci.scottsdale.az.us/parks /pinnacle*

Karabin, Marty. *Pinnacle Peak Rock Climbing Guide.* Phoenix, AZ: MK Productions, 2002.
Opland, Greg. *Phoenix Rock II.* Evergreen, CO: Chockstone Press, 1996.

Queen Creek
Tonto National Forest
2324 E. McDowell Rd.
Phoenix, AZ 85006
(602) 225-5200; *www.fs.fed.us/r3/tonto/home.html*

Karabin, Marty. *The Mine Area: Rock Climbing and Bouldering Guide.* Phoenix, AZ: MK Productions, 1998.

Karabin, Marty. *The Rock Jock's Guide to Queen Creek Canyon.* Phoenix, AZ: MK Productions, 1996.

Sedona
Coconino National Forest
Red Rock Ranger District
(928) 282-4119; *www.fs.fed.us/r3/coconino*

Bloom, David. *Castles in the Sand.* Boulder, CO: Sharp End Publishing, 2002.

Green, Stewart M. *Rockclimbing Arizona.* Helena, MT: Falcon Press, 1999.

Toula, Tim. *A Better Way to Die: Rock Climber's Guide to Sedona and Oak Creek Canyon.* Evergreen, CO: Chockstone Press, Inc., 1995.

Thumb Butte
Prescott National Forest
344 South Cortez St., Prescott, AZ 86303
(928) 443-8000; TTY (928) 443-8001; *www.fs.fed.us/r3/prescott/Green*

Baillie, Rusty. *Thumb Butte.* Prescott, AZ: Self-published, 1991.

Smith, Mike. *A Climber's Guide to Prescott, Arizona.* Prescott, AZ: Self-published, 2000.

B. ROUTES BY DIFFICULTY

5.0-5.3
Kreuser's Chimney Direct 5.3
South Crack 5.3
The Byrd 5.3
West Corner 5.1

5.4
Beginner
Dislocation Buttress
Kreuser's Route
Left of Sickle
Next to Nothing
The Chute
Unknown

5.5
Debut
Hanging Gardens
Jam on Jam
Quaker Oats
Ridgeback
Sinker
Slip N' Slide
Snorkeling in the Rhyolite
Unnamed
Unnamed

5.6
Baby Jr. Gets Spanked
Banana Split
Big and Loose
Boxcar Bob
Cat Claw
Christmas Chocolate
Circus Circus
Cruise Corner
Dislocation Direct
Duck Soup
Everday Five-Three
Fat Boy Goes to the Pond
Goliath
Green Horns to Green Dagger
Griffo
Heart Route

Hidden Chimney
Little Chimney Right
Magician
No Mystique
Normally Three Rurps
Obe Wan Kanobee
Ol' Solo Meo
One for the Road
Pocket Warmer
Progressive Slots
R-2 D-2
Rack and Pinyon
Sunshine Slab
Turtle Piss
Unnamed
Unnamed
Varicose
Worm
What's My Line 5.6 A0

5.7
Alley Oop
Barbeque Chips and Beer
Birthday Party
Chieu Hoi
Chutes and Ladders
Dead Meat
Easy Monday
Easy Money
Ego Trip
Follow Your Heart
Garbanzo Bean
Gingerbread
Grand Titon
Granite Jungle
Grunt 'N Dangle
Hiliter
Hitchcock
Hotdog in a Bun
Kitty Cracks
Lickety Split
Little Chimney Left

Live Oak
Lost Rupley Route
Mint Jam
Mixed Feelings
Nothing's Right
OK Corral
One Hard Move
Palo Verde
Queen Victoria
Renaissance Direct
R-Senio
Sharks Fin
The Classic
The Crawl
The Phantom
The Rigging
The Settlement
Treiber's Deception
Twin Cracks Left
Two Birds With One Stone
Unnamed
Water Drawn from an Ancient Well
We Be Jammin
Wide and Forgotten
Wind of Change

5.7+

South Face
Streaker Spire
Unknown Climb

5.8-

Hassayampa
Tread Gently

5.8

Anarchist's Delight
Angel's Delight
Ante Up
Applesticks
Bell Rock
Black Death
Bruisin' and Cruisin'
Burnt Buns
Bush Rush
Cakewalk
Chug-A-Lug

Couldn't Stand the Weather
Cut the Mustard
Delayed Flight
Driven by Fear
Hitchcock
I Sinkso
Jack Off
Jack Pot
Looking Sharp
Mars Attacks!
Mickey Mantle
Moby Dick
Mogenhead
Monday Morning Climb
Moon Floss
Morning's Mourning
Natural Wonder
Never to be the Same
Normally Urgent
Nothing's Left
Ojo Blanco
R-3
Red Wagon
Reunion
Sappy Love Song
Silhouette
Sissyboyz-8
Strawberry Razzle Tea
Sudden Impact
Sunday Stroll
Syzygy
The Classic
Turkey Franks
Twin Cracks Right
Unnamed
Yellow Edge

5.8+

Baby Jr.
Popeye Crack
R-1
Fire Zone

5.9-

Crackup
Magnolia Thunder Pussy
Warpath

5.9

Amateur Hour
Banana Crack
Beer and Dead Animals
Best Seller
Bet on Black
Betty Cracker
Charlie Don't Send
Chieu Hoi
Coatimundi Whiteout to
    Candyland
Corona Club
Double Or Nothin'
Dugald's Right
Face First
Fascist Pig
Forest Lawn
Four Flying Apaches
Glowing in the Distance
Goliath
Granite Jungle
Isaiah
Isle of You
Jack Frost
Let It Ride
Mary Jane
Maverick
Mecca
Mickey Goes to Vegas
Mint Julep
Naked Edge
Orange Out Direct
Paleface
Parental Guidance
Paul and Peggy's Route
Pickle Relish
Pomey Direct
R-4
Redemption
Sacred Datura Direct
Sheer Energy
Small Brown Mouse
Snap, Crack or Pop
Step Right Up
Trouble in Paradise
Unknown
Unknown
Walk in the Park
Y-Crack
You Don't Know Jack @#*!
Zenolith

5.9+

Asleep at the Wheel
Grasping for Straws
Riders on the Storm
The Mace

5.10a

Big Plans
Dealer's Choice
Dr. Sniff and the Tuna Boaters
Edge Your Bets
Fire Zone
Fist Full O Dollars
Jack's Crown
Jackson Five Ten
Jill and Drill
King of Pain
Loafer's Choice
One Armed Bandit
Out on Bail
Pocket Pulling Pansies on Parade
Pocket Puzzle
Saucy Jack
Slots O Fun
Sports Book
Stone Woman
The Cowboy
The New Comer
The Sickle
Two Cams and Jam

5.10b

Rupture
Unknown 5.10a/b

C. ROUTES BY QUALITY

★★★

Alley Oop 5.7
Amateur Hour 5.9
Angel's Delight 5.8
Best Seller 5.9
Burnt Buns 5.8
Chieu Hoi 5.7 or 5.9
Coatimundi Whiteout to
   Candyland 5.9
Crackup 5.9-
Dealer's Choice 5.10a
Debut 5.5
Dislocation Direct 5.6
Duck Soup 5.6
Forest Lawn 5.9
Four Flying Apaches 5.9
Gingerbread 5.7
Glowing in the Distance 5.9
Goliath 5.6 or 5.9
Hanging Gardens 5.5
Hotdog in a Bun 5.7
Isaiah 5.9
Loafer's Choice 5.10a
Looking Sharp 5.8
Magnolia Thunder Pussy 5.9-
Mars Attacks! 5.8
Mecca 5.9
Mickey Goes to Vegas 5.9
Moby Dick 5.8
Monday Morning Climb 5.8
Morning's Mourning 5.8
Naked Edge 5.9
One for the Road 5.6
Orange Out Direct 5.9
Pocket Puzzle 5.10a
Quaker Oats 5.5
R-1 5.8+
R-4 5.9
Renaissance Direct 5.7
Ridgeback 5.5
Sacred Datura Direct 5.9

Silhouette 5.8
Sinker 5.5
Slots O Fun 5.10a
South Crack 5.3
Sports Book 5.10a
Sunshine Slab 5.6
The Classic 5.7 or 5.8
The Mace 5.9+
The Sickle 5.10a
Treiber's Deception 5.7
What's My Line 5.6 A0
Yellow Edge 5.8
You Don't Know Jack @#*! 5.9

★★

Ante Up 5.8
Asleep at the Wheel 5.9+
Baby Jr. Gets Spanked 5.6
Beginner 5.4
Betty Cracker 5.9
Big and Loose 5.6
Birthday Party 5.7
Bruisin' and Cruisin' 5.8
Bush Rush 5.8
Chug-A-Lug 5.8
Chutes and Ladders 5.7
Circus Circus 5.6
Cruise Corner 5.6
Cut the Mustard 5.8
Dead Meat 5.7
Delayed Flight 5.8
Dr. Sniff and the Tuna Boaters
   5.10a
Driven by Fear 5.8
Dugald's Right 5.9
Edge Your Bets 5.10a
Ego Trip 5.7
Everday Five-Three 5.6
Face First 5.9
Follow Your Heart 5.7
Garbanzo Bean 5.7
Granite Jungle 5.7 or 5.9

Grasping for Straws 5.9+
Griffo 5.6
Grunt 'N Dangle 5.7
Hassayampa 5.8-
Heart Route 5.6
Isle of You 5.9
Jack Frost 5.9
Jack Off 5.8
Jackson Five Ten 5.10a
Jill and Drill 5.10a
Kitty Cracks 5.7
Left of Sickle 5.4
Mickey Mantle 5.8
Mint Jam 5.7
Mint Julep 5.9
Moon Floss 5.8
Never to be the Same 5.8
Next to Nothing 5.4
Normally Urgent 5.8
Nothing's Left 5.8
Nothing's Right 5.7
OK Corral 5.7
Ol' Solo Meo 5.6
One Armed Bandit 5.10a
Out on Bail 5.10a
Paleface 5.9
Pickle Relish 5.9
Pocket Pulling Pansies on Parade
    5.10a
Popeye Crack 5.8+
Progressive Slots 5.6
Queen Victoria 5.7
R-3 5.8
Red Wagon 5.8
Redemption 5.9
Sappy Love Song 5.8
Saucy Jack 5.10a
Sharks Fin 5.7
Sissyboyz-8 5.8
Slip N' Slide 5.5
Snorkeling in the Rhyolite 5.5
South Face 5.7+
Strawberry Razzle Tea 5.8
Streaker Spire 5.7+

Sunday Stroll 5.8
Syzygy 5.8
The Chute 5.4
The New Comer 5.10a
The Phantom 5.7
Tread Gently 5.8-
Trouble in Paradise 5.9
Twin Cracks Left 5.7
Twin Cracks Right 5.8
Two Birds With One Stone 5.7
Unknown 5.4
Unknown 5.9
Varicose 5.6
Walk in the Park 5.9
Warpath 5.9-
We Be Jammin 5.7
Wind of Change 5.7
Y-Crack 5.9

★

Applesticks 5.8
Baby Jr. 5.8+
Banana Crack 5.9
Barbeque Chips and Beer 5.7
Beer and Dead Animals 5.9
Bell Rock 5.8
Bet on Black 5.9
Big Plans 5.10a
Black Death 5.8
Boxcar Bob 5.6
Cakewalk 5.8
Charlie Don't Send 5.9
Christmas Chocolate 5.6
Corona Club 5.9
Couldn't Stand the Weather 5.8
Dislocation Buttress 5.4
Easy Monday 5.7
Easy Money 5.7
Fat Boy Goes to the Pond 5.6
Fire Zone 5.8+ or 5.10a
Fist Full O Dollars 5.10a
Grand Titon 5.7
Green Horns to Green Dagger 5.6
Hidden Chimney 5.6
Hiliter 5.7

Hitchcock 5.7 or 5.8
I Sinkso 5.8
Jack Pot 5.8
Jack's Crown 5.10a
King of Pain 5.10a
Kreuser's Chimney Direct 5.3
Kreuser's Route 5.4
Let It Ride 5.9
Lickety Split 5.7
Little Chimney Left 5.7
Little Chimney Right 5.6
Lost Rupley Route 5.7
Magician 5.6
Mary Jane 5.9
Maverick 5.9
Natural Wonder 5.8
No Mystique 5.6
Normally Three Rurps 5.6
Obe Wan Kanobee 5.6
Ojo Blanco 5.8
One Hard Move 5.7
Parental Guidance 5.9
Paul and Peggy's Route 5.9
Pocket Warmer 5.6
R-2 D-2 5.6
Rack and Pinyon 5.6
Reunion 5.8
Riders on the Storm 5.9+
R-Senio 5.7
Rupture 5.10b
Sheer Energy 5.9
Small Brown Mouse 5.9
Snap, Crack or Pop 5.9
Step Right Up 5.9
Stone Woman 5.10a
Sudden Impact 5.8

The Cowboy 5.10a
The Crawl 5.7
The Rigging 5.7
The Settlement 5.7
Turkey Franks 5.8
Turtle Piss 5.6
Unknown Climb 5.7+
Unnamed 5.8
Unnamed 5.5
Unnamed 5.6
Unnamed 5.5
Unnamed 5.6
Unnamed 5.7
Water Drawn from an Ancient Well
  5.7
West Corner 5.1
Wide and Forgotten 5.7
Zenolith 5.9

No stars

Anarchist's Delight 5.8
Banana Split 5.6
Cat Claw 5.6
Double Or Nothin' 5.9
Fascist Pig 5.9
Jam on Jam 5.5
Live Oak 5.7
Mixed Feelings 5.7
Mogenhead 5.8
Palo Verde 5.7
Pomey Direct 5.9
The Byrd 5.3
Two Cams and Jam 5.10a
Unknown 5.9
Unknown 5.10a/b
Worm 5.6

UIAA

The UIAA encourages the inclusion of information in guidebooks that helps visitors from overseas understand the most important information about local access, grades and emergency procedures. The UIAA also encourages climbers and mountaineers to share knowledge and views on issues such as safety, ethics, and good practice in mountain sports. The UIAA is not responsible for, and accepts no liability for, the technical content or accuracy of the information in this guidebook. Climbing, hill walking and mountaineering are activities with a danger of personal injury and death. Participants should be aware of, understand, and accept these risks and be responsible for their own actions and involvement.

INTERNATIONAL GRADE COMPARISON CHART

UIAA	USA	GB	F	D	AUS
V−	5.5	4a	5a	V	13
V	5.6	4b	5b	VI	14
V+	5.7	4c	5c	VI	14
VI−	5.8	4c	5c	VIIa	15
VI	5.9	5a	6a	VIIb	15
VI+	5.10a	5a	6a+	VIIc	16
VII−	5.10b	5b	6b	VIIIa	17
VII	5.10c	5b	6b+	VIIIb	18
VII+	5.10d	5c	6c	VIIIc	19
VIII−	5.11a	6a	6c+	IXa	20
VIII−	5.11b	6a	6c+	IXa	21
VIII	5.11c	6b	7a	IXb	22
VIII	5.11d	6b	7a	IXb	23
VIII+	5.12a	6b	7a+	IXc	24
IX−	5.12b	6c	7b	Xa	25
IX−	5.12c	6c	7b+	Xa	26
IX	5.12d	7a	7c	Xb	27
IX+	5.13a	7a	7c+	Xc	28
X−	5.13b	7b	8a	XIa	29
X−	5.13c	7b	8a+	XIa	30
X	5.13d	7b	8b	XIb	31
X+	5.14a	7b	8b+		32
XI−	5.14b	7b	8c		33
XI−	5.14c	7b	8c+		34
XI	5.14d	7b	9a		

Index

A

Alley Oop 5.7, 242
Amateur Hour 5.9, 242
Anarchist's Delight 5.8, 125
Angel's Delight 5.8, 242
Ante Up 5.8, 263
Applesticks 5.8, 244
Asleep at the Wheel 5.9+, 75

B

Baby Jr. 5.8+, 52
Baby Jr. Gets Spanked 5.6, 52
Banana Crack 5.9, 127
Banana Split 5.6, 125
Barbeque Chips and Beer 5.7, 147
Beer and Dead Animals 5.9, 107
Beginner 5.4, 162
Bell Rock 5.8, 225
Best Seller 5.9, 264
Bet on Black 5.9, 259
Betty Cracker 5.9, 268
Big and Loose 5.6, 183
Big Plans 5.10a, 264
Birthday Party 5.7, 119
Black Death 5.8, 137
Boxcar Bob 5.6, 90
Bruisin' and Cruisin' 5.8, 144
Burnt Buns 5.8, 247
Bush Rush 5.8, 250

C

Cakewalk 5.8, 138
Cat Claw 5.6, 127
Charlie Don't Send 5.9, 266
Chieu Hoi 5.7 or 5.9, 176
Christmas Chocolate 5.6, 102
Chug-A-Lug 5.8, 122
Chutes and Ladders 5.7, 122
Circus Circus 5.6, 259
Coatimundi Whiteout to
    Candyland 5.9, 172
Corona Club 5.9, 123
Couldn't Stand the Weather 5.8, 96

Crackup 5.9-, 247
Cruise Corner 5.6, 49
Cut the Mustard 5.8, 186

D

Dead Meat 5.7, 118
Dealer's Choice 5.10a, 260
Debut 5.5, 163
Delayed Flight 5.8, 117
Dislocation Buttress 5.4, 165
Dislocation Direct 5.6, 165
Double Or Nothin' 5.9, 259
Dr. Sniff and the Tuna Boaters
    5.10a, 73
Driven by Fear 5.8, 46
Duck Soup 5.6, 248
Dugald's Right 5.9, 248

E

Easy Monday 5.7, 96
Easy Money 5.7, 259
Edge Your Bets 5.10a, 258
Ego Trip 5.7, 139
Everday Five-Three 5.6, 241

F

Face First 5.9, 153
Fascist Pig 5.9, 125
Fat Boy Goes to the Pond 5.6, 101
Fire Zone 5.8+ or 5.10a, 77
Fist Full O Dollars 5.10a, 261
Follow Your Heart 5.7, 101
Forest Lawn 5.9, 34
Four Flying Apaches 5.9, 221

G

Garbanzo Bean 5.7, 150
Gingerbread 5.7, 241
Glowing in the Distance 5.9, 78
Goliath 5.6 or 5.9, 206
Grand Titon 5.7, 93
Granite Jungle 5.7 or 5.9, 175
Grasping for Straws 5.9+, 93
Green Horns to Green Dagger 5.6,
    165

Griffo 5.6, 251
Grunt 'N Dangle 5.7, 238

H

Hanging Gardens 5.5, 144
Hassayampa 5.8-, 169
Heart Route 5.6, 196
Hidden Chimney 5.6, 193
Hiliter 5.7, 114
Hitchcock 5.7 or 5.8, 60
Hotdog in a Bun 5.7, 186

I

I Sinkso 5.8, 139
Isaiah 5.9, 239
Isle of You 5.9, 51

J

Jack Frost 5.9, 264
Jack Off 5.8, 265
Jack Pot 5.8, 265
Jack's Crown 5.10a, 267
Jackson Five Ten 5.10a, 269
Jam on Jam 5.5, 123
Jill and Drill 5.10a, 267

K

King of Pain 5.10a, 125
Kitty Cracks 5.7, 183
Kreuser's Chimney Direct 5.3, 142
Kreuser's Route 5.4, 151

L

Left of Sickle 5.4, 188
Let It Ride 5.9, 262
Lickety Split 5.7, 145
Little Chimney Left 5.7, 184
Little Chimney Right 5.6, 184
Live Oak 5.7, 127
Loafer's Choice 5.10a, 118
Looking Sharp 5.8, 271
Lost Rupley Route 5.7, 67

M

Magician 5.6, 167
Magnolia Thunder Pussy 5.9-, 170
Mars Attacks! 5.8, 227
Mary Jane 5.9, 92
Maverick 5.9, 262
Mecca 5.9, 197
Mickey Goes to Vegas 5.9, 261

Mickey Mantle 5.8, 118
Mint Jam 5.7, 240
Mint Julep 5.9, 246
Mixed Feelings 5.7, 125
Moby Dick 5.8, 38
Mogenhead 5.8, 78
Monday Morning Climb 5.8, 194
Moon Floss 5.8, 94
Morning's Mourning 5.8, 246

N

Naked Edge 5.9, 115
Natural Wonder 5.8, 106
Never to be the Same 5.8, 78
Next to Nothing 5.4, 100
No Mystique 5.6, 73
Normally Three Rurps 5.6, 249
Normally Urgent 5.8, 244
Nothing's Left 5.8, 100
Nothing's Right 5.7, 101

O

Obe Wan Kanobee 5.6, 70
Ojo Blanco 5.8, 37
OK Corral 5.7, 50
Ol' Solo Meo 5.6, 98
One Armed Bandit 5.10a, 262
One for the Road 5.6, 136
One Hard Move 5.7, 189
Orange Out Direct 5.9, 247
Out on Bail 5.10a, 70

P

Paleface 5.9, 37
Palo Verde 5.7, 127
Parental Guidance 5.9, 143
Paul and Peggy's Route 5.9, 73
Pickle Relish 5.9, 186
Pocket Pulling Pansies on Parade
    5.10a, 102
Pocket Puzzle 5.10a, 102
Pocket Warmer 5.6, 103
Pomey Direct 5.9, 127
Popeye Crack 5.8+, 47
Progressive Slots 5.6, 262

Q

Quaker Oats 5.5, 139
Queen Victoria 5.7, 212

R

R-1 5.8+, 65
R-2 D-2 5.6, 70
R-3 5.8, 65
R-4 5.9, 67
Rack and Pinyon 5.6, 196
Red Wagon 5.8, 237
Redemption 5.9, 115
Renaissance Direct 5.7, 143
Reunion 5.8, 117
Riders on the Storm 5.9+, 98
Ridgeback 5.5, 80
R-Senio 5.7, 70
Rupture 5.10b, 118

S

Sacred Datura Direct 5.9, 149
Sappy Love Song 5.8, 101
Saucy Jack 5.10a, 270
Sharks Fin 5.7, 194
Sheer Energy 5.9, 65
Silhouette 5.8, 121
Sinker 5.5, 270
Sissyboyz-8 5.8, 77
Slip N' Slide 5.5, 148
Slots O Fun 5.10a, 259
Small Brown Mouse 5.9, 77
Snap, Crack or Pop 5.9, 269
Snorkeling in the Rhyolite 5.5, 89
South Crack 5.3, 121
South Face 5.7+, 40
Sports Book 5.10a, 259
Step Right Up 5.9, 269
Stone Woman 5.10a, 52
Strawberry Razzle Tea 5.8, 90
Streaker Spire 5.7+, 214
Sudden Impact 5.8, 77
Sunday Stroll 5.8, 272
Sunshine Slab 5.6, 189
Syzygy 5.8, 243

T

The Byrd 5.3, 98
The Chute 5.4, 136
The Classic 5.7 or 5.8, 172
The Cowboy 5.10a, 105
The Crawl 5.7, 163
The Mace 5.9+, 216

The New Comer 5.10a, 93
The Phantom 5.7, 142
The Rigging 5.7, 192
The Settlement 5.7, 152
The Sickle 5.10a, 188
Tread Gently 5.8-, 166
Treiber's Deception 5.7, 146
Trouble in Paradise 5.9, 66
Turkey Franks 5.8, 185
Turtle Piss 5.6, 123
Twin Cracks Left 5.7, 191
Twin Cracks Right 5.8, 191
Two Birds With One Stone 5.7, 78
Two Cams and Jam 5.10a, 127

U

Unknown 5.9, 53
Unknown 5.10a/b, 53
Unknown 5.4, 261
Unknown 5.9, 266
Unknown Climb 5.7+, 98
Unnamed 5.8, 62
Unnamed 5.5, 62
Unnamed 5.6, 62
Unnamed 5.5, 63
Unnamed 5.6, 63
Unnamed 5.7, 63

V

Varicose 5.6, 118

W

Walk in the Park 5.9, 271
Warpath 5.9-, 44
Water Drawn from an Ancient Well
    5.7, 147
We Be Jammin 5.7, 49
West Corner 5.1, 153
What's My Line 5.6 A0, 32
Wide and Forgotten 5.7, 48
Wind of Change 5.7, 78
Worm 5.6, 125

Y

Y-Crack 5.9, 122
Yellow Edge 5.8, 192
You Don't Know Jack @#*! 5.9, 269

Z

Zenolith 5.9, 125

About the Author

Lon Abbott has been climbing for 26 years and first became acquainted with Arizona rock in 1989. His love of mountains and rock climbing inspired him to become a geologist with a specialty in mountain-building processes. While doing graduate study and postdoctoral research at the University of California, Santa Cruz, he taught rock climbing classes. He has been a geology professor at Prescott College since 1997. Among the classes he teaches is Rock Climbing and Geology, which lends itself well to exploring the diverse geology and characteristics of Arizona climbing areas. Besides climbing, Lon enjoys pursuing his geologic research and spending time with his wife, Terri Cook, and two wonderful children, Logan and Kailas. Lon and Terri are coauthors of *Hiking the Grand Canyon's Geology*, published by The Mountaineers Books.

Lon Abbott with daughter Kailas

THE MOUNTAINEERS, founded in 1906, is a nonprofit outdoor activity and conservation club, whose mission is "to explore, study, preserve, and enjoy the natural beauty of the outdoors. . . ." Based in Seattle, Washington, the club is now the third-largest such organization in the United States, with seven branches throughout Washington State.

The Mountaineers sponsors both classes and year-round outdoor activities in the Pacific Northwest, which include hiking, mountain climbing, ski-touring, snowshoeing, bicycling, camping, kayaking, nature study, sailing, and adventure travel. The club's conservation division supports environmental causes through educational activities, sponsoring legislation, and presenting informational programs.

All club activities are led by skilled, experienced instructors, who are dedicated to promoting safe and responsible enjoyment and preservation of the outdoors.

If you would like to participate in these organized outdoor activities or the club's programs, consider a membership in The Mountaineers. For information and an application, write or call The Mountaineers, Club Headquarters, 300 Third Avenue West, Seattle, WA 98119; 206-284-6310. You can also visit the club's website at *www.mountaineers.org* or contact The Mountaineers via email at *clubmail@mountaineers.org*.

The Mountaineers Books, an active, nonprofit publishing program of the club, produces guidebooks, instructional texts, historical works, natural history guides, and works on environmental conservation. All books produced by The Mountaineers Books fulfill the club's mission.

Send or call for our catalog of more than 500 outdoor titles:

The Mountaineers Books
1001 SW Klickitat Way, Suite 201
Seattle, WA 98134
800-553-4453
mbooks@mountaineersbooks.org
www.mountaineersbooks.org

The Mountaineers Books is proud to be a corporate sponsor of The Leave No Trace Center for Outdoor Ethics, whose mission is to promote and inspire responsible outdoor recreation through education, research, and partnerships. The Leave No Trace program is focused specifically on human-powered (nonmotorized) recreation.

Leave No Trace strives to educate visitors about the nature of their recreational impacts, as well as offer techniques to prevent and minimize such impacts. Leave No Trace is best understood as an educational and ethical program, not as a set of rules and regulations.

For more information, visit *www.LNT.org*, or call 800-332-4100.

ESSENTIAL READING FOR CLIMBERS . . .

Mountaineering: The Freedom of the Hills, 7th Ed.
The Mountaineers Club
The all-time best selling standard reference for the sport of climbing.

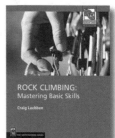

Rock Climbing: Mastering Basic Skills
Craig Luebben
For beginner to intermediate climbers.

Big Wall Climbing: Elite Technique
Jared Ogden
Skills and strategies unique to big walls.

Gym Climbing: Maximizing Your Indoor Experience
Matt Burbach
Urban climbing for new climbers, climbers staying in shape and climbers who find all the challenge they desire indoors.

Climbing: Training for Peak Performance
Clyde Soles
Build the muscles you need for this ultimate of muscle-powered sports.

Mountain Weather: Backcountry Forecasting & Weather Safety for Hikers, Campers, Climbers, Skiers, Snowboarders
Jeff Renner
Written by a weatherman with a fixation for outdoor sports—he's got this topic covered.